The Edges of Fiction

T0056401

The Edges of Fiction

Jacques Rancière

Translated by Steve Corcoran

polity

First published in French as *Les bords de la fiction* © Editions du Seuil, 2017
Collection *La Librairie du XXIe siècle*, sous la direction de Maurice Olender

Polity Press
65 Bridge Street
Cambridge CB2 1UR, UK

Polity Press
101 Station Landing
Suite 300
Medford, MA 02155, USA

ISBN-13: 978-1-5095-3044-1
ISBN-13: 978-1-5095-3045-8 (pb)

A catalogue record for this book is available from the British Library.

Names: Ranciere, Jacques, author.
Title: The edges of fiction / Jacques Ranciere.
Other titles: Bords de la fiction. English
Description: Medford, MA : Polity, 2019. | First published in French as Les bords de la fiction (Paris : Editions du Seuil, 2017). | Includes bibliographical references and index.
Identifiers: LCCN 2019981534 (print) | LCCN 2019016715 (ebook) | ISBN 9781509530441 (hardback) | ISBN 9781509530458 (paperback) | ISBN 9781509530472 (epub)
Subjects: LCSH: Fiction. | Fiction--History and criticism--Theory, etc. | BISAC: LITERARY CRITICISM / Semiotics & Theory.
Classification: LCC PN3331 .R25713 2019 (ebook) | LCC PN3331 (print) | DDC 808.3--dc23
LC record available at https://lccn.loc.gov/2019981534

Typeset in 11 on 13pt Sabon
by Fakenham Prepress Solutions, Fakenham, Norfolk NR21 8NL
Printed and bound in Great Britain by TJ International Limited

For further information on Polity, visit our website: politybooks.com

Contents

Acknowledgements

I wish to thank everyone who has provided impetus to this work and enabled me to outline its themes and contours. My gratitude goes first to Azucena González Blanco and Erika Martínez, organizers of a conference on 'The Politics of Literature' held in Granada in December 2014. I was able to pursue and discuss my reflections thanks to the invitations I received from various institutions: the University of California in Los Angeles and in Irvine, the Academy of Beaux-Arts in Düsseldorf, the Fondation Gulbenkian in Paris, the University of Toulouse-Jean Jaurès, the Monokl publishing house in Istanbul, the Philosophia festival in Saint-Émilion and the National University of Valparaiso. The talk I gave at Irvine was published as 'Fictions of Time' in a collective volume, *Rancière and Literature*, edited by Grace Hellyer and Julian Murphet.

'The Edges of Fiction' ('Les bords de la fiction') was the title first given to a talk held at the Fondation Gulbenkian in February 2016 and published by that institution. A first version of the chapter titled 'The Unimaginable' was published, in 2014, in a special issue of the *Cahier de l'Herne* on Joseph Conrad, edited by Josiane Paccaud-Huguet and Claude Maisonnat.

A first version of the chapter 'The Random Moment' came out as 'The Politics of Fiction' and, together with a picture by Alfredo Jaar, comprised issue No. 3 of *L'Estacio*, published in Barcelona in May 2016.

All the other chapters of this book have never before been published.

Introduction

What distinguishes fiction from ordinary experience is not a lack of reality but a surfeit of rationality. That is the thesis formulated by Aristotle in the ninth chapter of the *Poetics*. Poetry, by which he means the construction of dramatic or epic fictions, is 'more philosophical' than history because the latter says only how things happen, one after the other, in their particularity, whereas poetic fiction says how things *can* happen in general. Events do not occur in it at random. They occur as the necessary or verisimilar consequences of a chain of causes and effects. Such a chain can be shown to produce the most general determinations of human existence – the fact of knowing happiness or misfortune, and of going from one to the other. This chain is no longer a fatality imposed by a divine power. It is inherent to the order of human action and to the relation it entertains with knowledge. Fictional reason carried out exactly this revolution: the tragic hero's misfortune is no longer a condition to be endured but instead the consequence of an error – of some error or other in the conduct of one's action and no longer a transgression of the divine order. And this misfortune occurs through a specific mode of causality.

Indeed, this causal chain cannot be defined by rigour alone. Its effect must also be contrary to that which we are led to expect. The proper chain of causes and effects is attested by the reversal – the peripeteia – it produces in the universe of expectations. The rationality of fiction is that appearances – or expectations, for in Greek the same word expresses both things – are inverted. It is that one state leads to the inverse state and that, by the same token, something one was unaware of comes to be known. Prosperity and misfortune, the expected and the unexpected, ignorance and knowledge – these three oppositions form the stable matrix of classic fictional reason in the West. The overall chain articulating them, says Aristotle, has two modalities: it can be necessary or verisimilar. However, practice shows that verisimilitude is charged with proving necessity.

The importance of the theoretical matrix thus constructed must not be overlooked. This model of fictional rationality is by no means limited in its principle to the inventions of poets. Its field of application can be extended to wherever what is at stake is to show the linking of causes and effects that leads beings, unbeknownst to themselves, from happiness to misfortune, or from misfortune to happiness. Our contemporaries no longer write tragedies in verse. Yet one may easily verify that even today the Aristotelian principles of fictional rationality form the stable matrix of the knowledge that our societies produce about themselves. In the great theories of society and history, as well as in the short-sighted, day-to-day oracular science of politicians, experts, journalists or essayists, the matter is still one of developing the chain of causality that leads us, has led us or will lead us to fortune or to misfortune. Accordingly, it is still a matter of showing how these causes produce their effects by inverting appearances and expectations, how prosperity awaits us at the end of an endured ordeal, or disaster at the end of illusions of happiness. It is thus a matter of showing how misfortune is the effect of an ignorance that is itself an object of knowledge. It is lastly a matter of showing all this within a discursive figure that equates necessity and verisimilitude. Marx, Freud and Braudel have taught us as much, each in their own way: the good science of human actions and conducts is recognizable in its faithfulness to the fundamental structures of fictional rationality – the distinguishing of temporalities, the relationship between the known and the unknown, and the paradoxical chain of causes and effects. If the Bachelardian formula of scientific rationality, 'There is science only of the hidden', is so very similar to the reasoning of detective Rouletabille, it is because both share a common origin in the Aristotelian principle of paradoxical causality: truth is established as an inversion of what appearances have led us to expect.

This reminder aims to demonstrate not that everything is fiction and that nothing has changed since Aristotle. By contrast, it enables us to gauge the transformations of fictional rationality that social science and literature carried out in the modern era in the West. To be able to apply the principles of the Aristotelian fictional order to the entire gamut of human events, a contradiction indeed had to be resolved. This causal rationality contrasted with the empirical succession of facts to the extent that it restricted its domain of application. It concerned action, the errors that agents commit in carrying it out, and the unforeseen effects its unfolding produces. But causal rationality was thereby the sole preserve of those who acted and expected something to come from their action. Some will say that a great number of people were thus included! But the contrary is true. In bygone days it was the accepted consensus that the number of these subjects is restricted, since most humans, properly speaking, do not act: they make objects or children, execute orders or render services, and continue doing the next day what they had done the day before. Nowhere does any expectation or reversal arise, nor do any errors made enable one to pass from one condition to the opposite. Classical fictional rationality therefore concerned a very small number of humans and human activities. The remainder were subject to anarchy, to the empirical real's absence of cause. This is why one could, in the positive sense of the term, ignore it: not deal with it, not seek to provide it with a rationale.

In its classical form, the rationality of fiction thus implies a twofold relationship of knowledge to ignorance. Fictional knowledge arranges the events by which active men go from fortune to misfortune and from ignorance to knowledge. But this knowledge is itself deployed only by ignoring – by treating as negligible – the mass of beings and situations belonging to the repetitive universe of material things and events that happen simply one after the other, without creating expectations or forcing errors, and thus without ever going through those reversals of fortune that give the universe of fictional actions its rationality. At most this fictional order reserved, as in comedy, a minor place for the ordinary stories that happened to people of no importance, leaving in its margins the mixture of conditions and upheavals occurring without rhyme or reason that characterized the novel, which was made for amusement and not to gain any knowledge.

This distribution of knowledge and ignorance was overturned in the modern age. But the forms of this overturning must be clarified. According to dominant opinion, this age is one that made a clear-cut separation between, on the one hand, the science of real relations, at long last freed from the artifices of fiction and, on the other, literature and art, at long last freed from the constraints of the real and its imitation. But it is rather the contrary that is true: the essential process founding modern literature and social science simultaneously is the abolition of the division in which the fictional rationality of plots is opposed to the empirical succession of facts. Modern literature and social science both challenge the separation between the rationale of fiction and that of ordinary facts. But they do so in two opposite ways.

On the one hand, social science adopted the Aristotelian principles of fictional rationality for its own account, while abolishing the boundaries delimiting their field of validity. The dark world of material activities and daily facts admits of the same rationality as the arrangements of tragic action – this is the founding axiom of modern social science. This science even took a step further when, with Marx, it asserted the strict reversal of the old hierarchy: it is in the dark world of productive activity that the principle of rationality governing societies resides. The incredible feats of princes, which had nourished the major forms of fiction, are only the surface effects of this dark world. The world of things and people of whom nothing was known – i.e. who were disregarded – as a matter of convention becomes the true world. But this elevation has its strict setback. The dark world becomes the true world as a world whose truth is not known in another sense – that is, is misjudged – by those who live in it. All told, the true world of modern social science is the tragic world democratized, in which all share the privilege of error. This science thus brings both types of ignorance to coincide. It simply reserves all knowledge concerning the paradoxical chain and the inversion of appearances for itself alone.

Literature, for its part, took the opposite path. Instead of democratizing Aristotelian fictional reason in order to include all human activity in the world of rational knowledge, it destroyed the principles of this reason, abolishing the limits that circumscribed a real specific to fiction. Literature was doubtless the first to affirm, in the times of Balzac and of Hugo, the story-power carried by the scenery and forms of daily life. However, it turned this power inherent to ordinary things, beings and events, into the principle of a departure from the great schemas of transition from fortune to misfortune and from ignorance to knowledge. The two great interpreters of the modern novel's developments, namely Georg Lukács and Erich Auerbach, both registered this gap, in some sense despite themselves. The former celebrated, in the Balzacian novel, the coming together of the fictional rationality of action and the scientific rationality of the historical process. As Lukács says to us, Lucien de Rubempré's and his peers' grand, disastrous endeavours reveal to us the nascent ascendency of capitalism. But this paradise of concordant rationalities is soon lost. Passing from the theatre in *Lost Illusions* to that in *Nana*, the novel then mires narrative action in the static description of reified social relationships. As a good Marxist, Lukács might have thought it normal that, like so many other ideals, the aristocratic logic of action was drowning in the 'icy waters of egotistical calculation'. He will prefer to conclude, as an inconsistent Marxist, that it was the novelists who had abdicated by abandoning the narration of actions for the description of things.

Auerbach, for his part, gets to the nub of the problem: the novelistic revolution entails the negation of what had founded the intelligibility of the old fiction, which is to say the separation of forms of life, the separation between humans living in the time of causality and those living in the time of the chronicle. For him, the history of novelistic realism becomes a conjunction of two processes: one that integrates any event into the totality of a social process and one that turns any individual, as humble as they may be, into a 'serious' subject of fiction, a character capable of the most intense and complex feelings. But the promised conjunction slips away at the critical moment. The antepenultimate chapter of *Mimesis* announces that, in Stendhal's time, the western novel attained its essential achievement, which consists in 'representing man engaged only in a global political, economic and social reality in constant evolution'.[1] But the statement is forthwith belied by Auerbach's illustrating this 'constantly evolving global reality' with the closed and desperately motionless universe of the hôtel de la Mole, the Maison Vauquer and Emma Bovary's dining room. Indeed, the last chapter effects a remarkable reversal and ends up celebrating empty and disconnected time, with Auerbach seeing western realism's supreme achievement as the conquest of the random moment, unrelated to any continuity of action.

What Lukács denies and Auerbach encounters without thematizing it is this scission of fictional rationality. The individual engaged in the global reality of a history in constant evolution and the random individual capable of the most intense and complex feelings do not comprise the same subject. Social science would seize upon the former, the price to pay for which is a different reconstitution of the hierarchy of forms of time and the logic of paradoxical linking. Literature would tie itself to the latter. It tore down the barrier that separated lives without hi/story from lives apt to encounter the vicissitudes of fortune and the uncertainties of knowledge. It thus challenged the major forms of articulation of time and causality that had structured Aristotelian fiction and that structure expert accounts on society today. This it did to plumb the power of the 'random occurrence', this empty occurrence hanging in the balance between the reproduction of the same and the possible emergence of the new, and which is also a full moment in which an entire life is condensed, in which several forms of time mix together and in which the inactivity of a reverie enters into harmony with the activity of the universe. Using this temporal frame, it built other ways of identifying events and actors, and other ways of linking them to construct shared worlds and shared hi/stories.

For whether it is in the avowed fictions of literature or in the unavowed fictions of politics, social science or journalism, the matter is still one of constructing through sentences the perceptible and thinkable forms of a shared world by determining situations and their actors, by identifying events, by establishing among them links of coexistence or succession, and by giving to these links the modality of the possible, the real or the necessary. The prevailing custom nevertheless sets these two sides in opposition. It gives to the fictions of social or political science the attributes of reality and analyses the forms of avowed fiction as effects or distorted reflections of this reality. I have challenged this division in various works, whether by showing that literature itself created the interpretive schemas applied by social science to the forms of literary fiction, or by studying the fashion in which literature has subverted the categories of action and the logic of verisimilitude.[2] For all that, the point is not to announce an inversion whereby social science's transformations can be deduced from those of literature. It is legitimate, by contrast, to restore all heuristic value to the transformations of fictional rationality, and notably to the transformations of forms of subject constitution and forms for identifying events and constructing shared worlds specific to the modern literary revolution. At a time when the mediocre fiction called 'information' purports to saturate the field of what is actual, with its hackneyed feuilletons about petty go-getters out to conquer power, backdropped by big-time scoops about faraway atrocities, such research can usefully contribute to broadening the horizon of gazes at, and thoughts about, what gets called a world and the ways of inhabiting it.

The book's four parts aim to contribute some elements to this investigation into fiction's transformations. They variously analyse modern fiction's constitutive movement: the movement by which its centre of gravity was shifted from its traditional core, constituted by the knot of narrative events, toward those edges in which fiction is confronted with its possible cancellation, or returned to such and such a figure of alterity. These are, first, the edges at which fiction receives the world of beings and situations formerly relegated to the margins: the trivial events of daily life or the bruteness of a real that does not permit of inclusion. These are also situations in which the difference between that which happens and that which simply goes-by tends to be erased. These are, further, the uncertain boundaries between events that one reports and those that one invents. These are thus also the ways in which fiction is divided from within, in which it modifies its linkages and invents, as needed, new genres to retrace the boundary or else to duly note its erasure. These are, lastly, the edges at which the account that means to document the real, and the science that seeks to reveal its hidden truth, appropriate avowed fiction in one form or another.

The first part examines the transformations of the frame within which fiction delimits and peoples a specific sensible world. To do this, it sets out from the somewhat simplistic figuration given to this frame in the century following the French Revolution: one of a world in which, at one and the same time, the closed windows that separated fiction's characters and situations of choice from prosaic reality are opened, and the barriers that had separated the classes and their worlds crumble. It shows how this scenario complexifies, as the vast space in which the new novel dreamt of identifying itself with the encyclopaedia of social space shrinks down to the enigma of a face behind a closed window, or gets lost in the infinity of reveries occasioned by a landscape, an uncertain light or hour; or as the imagination, believing it can enter into any passing body in the street, encounters bodies in their evasiveness, locking their secrets safely away and shattering the very frames that enable shared experience to be recounted.

The second part shows how the rationality of the story and that of science converge in a bid to reveal not only the reality causing an appearance but also the cause of which that reality itself is the effect. In this way, scientific demonstration, the fantasy story, documentary inquiry and historical narration must all come together to express the secret of the commodity. In the same period, science and story knot together differently when the detective novel renovates causal rationality, which stands threatened by the distended time of the realist novel, but in so doing pays the price of oscillating between two models of science and of having its causality split from within.

The third part ponders the meaning and forms that fictional imagination takes when the barriers that had separated the logic of facts and the logic of fictions vanish: when a novelist, convinced that genuine imagination never invents anything, must nevertheless do just that and has characters he has never 'encountered' go into action; or when the chronicle of a journey, the stages of which are precisely set out on a map, leaves us uncertain as to the type of reality being related to us at each stage and as to the journey's very temporality.

The fourth part enquires – in the wake of a renowned commentator – into the community that fiction sketches and into the humanity that it promises when it ceases to be the arrangement of actions with which so many centuries had identified it. To this end, it explores the limit fictions which include those to whom nothing normally can or ought to happen or which sit on the very line of separation between the world in which nothing happens and that in which something takes place.

The attentive reader may naturally verify that, thus defined, causal linking simply proves to be one order among others and that each episode of this hi/story crosses the borders by which the chapters and parts are delimited, and thus enters into resonance with this or that other one, reprising its problems and re-examining its objects and stakes. Each chapter and part is, in sum, the account of a singular intellectual adventure that comes to be reflected in the others and reflects them in its turn, in accordance with the egalitarian principle which reflection on intellectual emancipation opposes to the precepts of progressive – in both senses of the word – pedagogy. The same reader will easily verify that these investigations into the modern adventures of fictional rationality also variously reverberate with others that I have devoted to adventures of the sensible, adventures in which new subjects are constituted, shared worlds formed and conflicts emerge between worlds: in which words become flesh and divert lives from their destination, nights shake up the normal cycle of day and night, and gazes through windows engender the division of proletarian bodies; in which mutilated statues, flea-ridden children or capering clowns create a new beauty, and the groping for knowledge of the ignorant as they face signs of writing defines another life of intelligence. Through all these adventures, what is pursued is one and the same inquiry into the revolution by which those who are nothing become everything.

Doors and Windows

Behind the Windows

In 1857 the literary critic Armand de Pontmartin wrote his review of *Madame Bovary*. To the realist overload of little people and vulgar things bogging down the novel of provincial mores, he opposes the happy times when fiction's object bore on the delicate feelings of men and women of quality. People of this latter sort gazed upon the countryside and ordinary people only from afar, through their palace windows or their carriage doors. These windows separating social classes from one another also separated novelistic fiction from ordinary reality. They could thereby open 'a large, admirably filled, space for the analysis of feelings, subtler, more complicated, more difficult to unravel in elite souls than among common people'.[1] In democratic times doors and windows were allegedly too wide open, thus allowing onto the whiteness of pages, along with mud from the countryside, the triviality of little people and the clutter of paltry things.

Nothing is served by denouncing the aristocratic prejudice of this journalist with his nobiliary particle. His prejudice goes without saying. But neither is it necessary to admire, as was done not so long ago, the lucidity of reactionary writers and critics supposedly able 'despite their prejudice' to show us the reality of class struggle. For them, this struggle also went without saying. It is therefore not despite their prejudices but because of them that they set their objective at the precise point where the topography of a fictional world opens not simply onto social reality but onto the symbolic topography that renders it visible and in which everyone is assigned their place. Exactly this is what the critic's allusion to windows and doors symbolizes. It is clearly understood that he speaks through metaphor. But metaphor is something other than the use of imagery to express a thought. It is, far more profoundly, a way of inscribing the description of a state of things into the symbolic topography that determines the forms of its visibility. Our critic does precisely this. He may hanker after the good old times of social and novelistic aristocracy. Yet he remains of his time, which is that of modern political and aesthetic revolutions. And during this time critique changes its status. No longer does it say how works should be – or should have been – made to satisfy the rules of art and the public's taste. It says how they are made, what sensible world they construct, and how they reflect the spirit of the times that engenders them. Pontmartin follows suit. He does not say that Flaubert's novel is ill conceived or poorly written. He says that it is similar to its time, that of democracy, is animated by the energy of this brutal historical force and, like it, drags along, in its flow, all sorts of detritus. Saying this requires him to fix on descriptions of states of things or on sensations that admit of being transformed into open windows overlooking the reality whose product they are. He thus turns the novel itself into a door open onto the world that engendered it.

For there are two sorts of doors and windows in fiction. Those that fiction describes and that serve the ends of narration: doors through which one goes to engage in this or that activity, or against which one stumbles, like a barrier that fences in the elected being or keeps apart social conditions; windows of yesterday's picaresque fictions in through which young people climbed using makeshift ladders; the new windows of sentimental fictions, those behind which young women grew bored but also, occasionally, would fix their eyes on an unexpected sight that would turn their lives upside down. But fiction also has unstated doors and windows: such are novel openings that set down not only the elements of a plot but also the very texture of a world of beings, things and events and its (dis)continuous relationship with the so-called real world; such are also descriptions that not only portray the setting of an action but also set in place a world of visibility in harmony or in rupture with the relation-ships established between things and words in the usual order of the world. And, of course, the windows and doors that serve as accessories to fiction can themselves always become metaphors of fiction's modes of visibility and forms of linking, of the type of real it constructs and the type of reality that makes it possible.

Pontmartin's metaphor moves in this space. But, like the reactionaries of his time, he hurries unduly to make an opposition between yesterday's elite with their grand spaces and noble perspectives and the democratic age's cluttered spaces and muddy paths. This hurriedness means he is unable to form a more precise view of fiction's transformations or define them more exactly relative to the transformations affecting social divides. For, between yesteryear's protective windows and his era's wide open doors, inordinately many events have, in truth, taken place which his grid cannot retain. The doors that enabled the elites to keep a distance from commonplace lives were followed by other doors, ones that kept commonplace life at a distance from the hidden secrets of souls and of society. Windows proved to be apposite at drawing souls together, just as they had been at keeping different social conditions apart. By themselves they blurred the relations between inside and outside, noble and vulgar, whether by submitting the salons of the elite to the gaze of entomological science or by offering to the gaze of the artist or the lover the poetry of society's dark face. They created new affects, muddling the hierarchy of passions, the aetiology of their causes, the forms of their expression and their assignation to this or that social condition. They thus rendered uncertain not only the boundaries between conditions but also the very divisions between contemplation and action, the fictive and the real.

The simple division established by the aristocratic critic is gainsaid, first, by the discovery that, behind the doors and windows of palaces, the so-called elite souls are divided into two irreconcilable categories. There are those who, by choosing to conceal their feelings and lock up their fellows, reveal their effective baseness, and there are those who side with the windows, who take the side of transparency and sincerity. From one window to another, these latter, nobly natured souls recognize each other and set apart their sensitive nobility from all matters of social conditions. Stendhal's characters bear witness to this. The shared singularity of *The Charterhouse of Parma* and *The Red and the Black* is that their respective heroes are afforded a stay behind prison walls that is experienced as a moment of absolute happiness: in prison this hero is indifferent to society's vain intrigues, able to discover the only good that counts – commerce with a soul of the same nature. Locked up in the old-style prison at Besançon, Julien Sorel can relive – removed from any social ambition or humiliation – his pure love for Madame de Rênal. As for Fabrizio, he is imprisoned in a fortress that no one can visit and where a conscientious general has ordered a wooden shutter to be built to block his view to the outside. Prior to the carpentry's completion, however, Fabrizio has enough time to discover, six feet lower and twenty-five feet away, the aviary where, every day, the tyrant's daughter Clélia comes to tend her birds. Thus, he has enough time to see the young lady peer up at his dungeon window with the sort of compassion-filled look that, since Rousseau, has expressed not only sympathy for those who suffer but also a recognition of the suffering person as a fellow creature – one sensitive soul recognizing a soul of the same nature. The certainty acquired in this distant exchange of gazes gives Fabrizio the energy he needs to cut an opening in the heavy woodwork so that the dialogue of gazes may continue. This certainty will imbue these two young people with the ingenuity they require to be able to communicate in signs and later in words made from letters cut out of makeshift alphabets. Such is how the two noble souls inhabiting the prison, run by the 'liberal' Conti on behalf of a contemptible local potentate, can recognize each other from one window to another.

The reader may greet the ease of this recognition with scepticism. How could the hero cut a hole in the wooden shutter using only a watch spring? How can we believe that this faint opening sufficed for these young people to exchange increasingly lengthy and compli-cated messages over such a distance? But this request for verisimilitude is not simply beside the point. It also implies a judgement on the person who makes it, placing them alongside the jailers who track down sensitive souls. These latter know precisely neither obstacles nor objections. Their transparency is not subject to the chance of circumstance. It was on the main road near the town that the two young individuals first met, and that Fabrizio, standing at the door of Clélia's coach, formed a seemingly unbecoming judgement concerning the young girl, twelve years old at the time: 'She'd be a charming companion in prison. What deep thoughts must lie behind that brow of hers! She would know how to love.'[2] As to the three-year idyll that the lovers will enjoy upon Fabrizio's release, it will unfold entirely in the dark. The official reason we are given is that Clélia is keeping her solemn promise to the Madonna: never to *see* the one she loves again. As the Madonna is unlikely to have appreciated Clélia's keeping her promise in this way while also cheating on her husband, we must certainly consider that the real reason for this remaining in the dark lies elsewhere: those who recognize each other at first glance no longer need to see each other. For his part, the novelist has nothing further to say about these lovers, no longer separated by any wall, and so asks the reader's permission to pass in silence over their three years of bliss.

The proximity of souls through distant windows breaks with the old narrative hierarchy. However, this rupture by no means tallies with the division of old and new times invoked by the nostalgic critic. Even if Stendhal suggests that the true father of the youngest son of the marquis del Dongo is an officer of Republican France, this does not make of Fabrizio the representative of a democracy invading the space formerly reserved for elite souls. The turmoil introduced into the aristocratic world of feelings and actions does not rest on the invasion of the masses but on the regime of the visible established with this story of communication at a distance. And this regime attests to a singular blurring of times. For this recognition of souls through the language of eyes and attitudes seems more a harking back to the past than a gesture toward the future. It harks back to that eighteenth century in

which an equality among sensitive souls was invented
that thwarts at once accidents of birth and the artifices
of those who try to disguise its effects. Fabrizio and
Clélia recognize each other as do sensitive Rousseauian
souls who refuse any distance between social conditions, or as does Voltaire's aristocrat, seduced by the
simplicity of his servant Nanine. But they also recognize
each other in the manner of those masters who, in
Marivaux, very quickly recognize each other beneath
their valet-and-servant disguises, thanks to which each
believes themselves able to observe covertly the true
nature of their betrothed. They recognize each other
as sensitive beings whose eyes and gestures cannot but
express their nature, and as reasonable beings who,
in the age of ideology and languages of signs, are
never short of means for making their feelings known.
Despite the distance and inconvenience of the spatial
arrangement, the lovers' communication between prison
windows never gives rise to a misunderstanding or loss
of information. For these windows metaphorize the
relationship between two souls given to each other as
two entirely transparent surfaces on which feelings are
expressed in their eyes, gestures and attitudes, without
loss or feigning. This is also why this kind of commerce
through eyes and souls is shielded from espionage.
Surveillance by the small-minded cannot catch communication among sensitive souls unawares, for a very
simple reason: this surveillance and this communication
are not part of the same world. To recognize each
other, sincere souls require only the smallest square of
day. Consequently, the power of jailers is exhausted
by hermetically sealing this square, preventing their
gazes from crossing. This power is thwarted when the
least sliver of light exists by which they are able to do
so. These transparent windows are perhaps the final
form of the utopia of sincere souls that had traversed

the preceding century and whose indelible imprint the young Beyle transmitted to the novelist Stendhal.

Stendhal thought that only people from the future would understand him. But he mistook the reason why: what was valuable about the idyll behind the prison windows in Parma, what ensured its later success, was not that its psychology was ahead of its time. It was, on the contrary, its perfect anachronism. By the time of Balzac and Flaubert, direct communication between sensitive souls had become a thing of the past. Or, rather, it had become divided between two extremes: on the one side, it had become submerged in the telepathic universe of Swedenborgian spirituality; on the other, it had been turned into a seducer's cliché, good only for catching sentimental provincials, such as Dinah Piédefer (*The Muse of the Department*) or Emma Bovary.

Of course, both these sides enter into communication with one another, but the price to be paid is the rather brutal introduction of the supernatural into the everyday universe. *Ursule Mirouet* provides the perfect example of this. Balzac wrote this work shortly after having read *The Charterhouse of Parma*, and he surely recalled Fabrizio and Clélia when he begot, with a single glance through a window, the passion of the young Ursule for Savinien de Portenduère. But the two gazes that meet in his novel are not those of souls who recognize each other from afar, across a penal space keeping them apart. Able to see her neighbour's large open window through her own open window, the young provincial woman instead admires the young Parisian for the elegance of his gestures and toilette accessories. And if both souls come together at the end, it is thanks to a completely different way of seeing at a distance. It is telepathy that enables a Swedenborgian to describe accurately to Ursule's incredulous godfather what happens in the young lady's room in his absence.

Telepathy will also enable Ursule, later on, to see her dead godfather appear in her dreams and discover with him the theft her cousin has perpetrated against her. It is thanks to this rather prosaic use of communication among minds that the young woman is able to recover her fortune and marry the young man seen through the window opposite. We thus see why, in the lengthy praise of *The Charterhouse* he was writing up at the same time, Balzac omitted to mention the dialogue of sincere souls between two windows. These openings, through which transparent souls recognize their fellows, have become opaque for him. This is not because in Balzac's work windows have lost their importance. Quite the contrary: windows serve to get the story underway on more than one occasion. Yet souls no longer meet through these openings. Windows have become frames that block sight and form an apparatus of capture. This apparatus first assumes the face of an entomological gaze that grasps the characters of various social species. But this clear visibility soon muddies, and the hunter himself becomes captive, as when the frame cuts from a tableau of social species the image of a new idol, or when the gaze loses itself in the indistinctness of reverie.

This capture first takes place from a neutral vantage point – the street of anonymous pedestrians. And it targets in particular the elite beings who do not deign to cast their gaze on the vulgarity of life outside. In *The Collection of Antiquities*, Balzac tasks the journalist Émile Blondet with evoking his childhood reminiscences of the four-corner windows through which passers-by could see, as in a glass cage, the powdered automatons populating the Esgrignon family's dining room: 'Peeping in through the window-panes, I gazed at the battered bodies, and ill-jointed limbs (how they were fastened together, and, indeed, their whole anatomy was a mystery I never attempted to explain); I saw the lantern jaws, the protuberant bones, the abnormal development of the hips.'[3] Those who aristocratically turn their backs to the vulgarities of the outside have become caged animals or automatons in a window display. This is not a particularity of the provincial streets of Alençon. It is, far more generally, about the new novel's inversion of the old paths going from inside to outside. The new novel does more, however: it identifies the point of view of the passer-by casting a curious eye through the window with that of the expert identifying a dying social species. The window is a museum display case, in which those who attempt to withdraw and distance themselves from the modern world are offered up to observation as objects of science.

This threat clearly meets with a simple riposte: one may close one's curtains and tuck oneself away in the tightly shut apartments of seldom-frequented neighbourhoods. In this way, *A Second Home* describes the pious zeal of another native of Lower Normandy, the young Madame de Granville, that leads her to cloister her family life at the bottom of the Marais. This measure is nonetheless taken in vain, as it results in her husband's having to pass through the narrow streets of working-class areas to get to work. The young magistrate thus becomes exposed to the power of other windows – those that make the darkness of winding streets communicate with that of working-class dwellings. At the hour when apartment lamps are lit, these windows make it possible to grasp no longer a particular social species but the other side of society – the world of work and poverty. But they offer it to the gaze in a quite specific form: as a vision of fugitive art, as a genre painting in which, as with Diderot, the painting's charm is inseparable from the moral of its subject – a mother and her daughter at work embroidering by the light of a lamp concentrated by two globes of glass, seated behind iron bars up which the young worker's nasturtiums, sweet pea and convolvulus have climbed.[4] In truth, the moral of the tableau quickly reveals itself to be a mere stage on the path of vice: the mother and daughter will not need to be asked twice to accept the passer-by's solicitations and swap the dark dwelling in the rue du Tourniquet-Saint-Jean for an apartment on the Chaussée-d'Antin, where the young needleworker lives as a kept woman. But the main point does not lie therein. It lies in the twofold upheaval of fictional hierarchy performed by these windows with a street view, windows that transform aristocrats into animals on display in a natural history museum and, conversely, change the faces of workers bent over their work into visions of art and objects of love.

This use of windows gives the democratization of fiction a somewhat more complex figure than is offered by Armand de Pontmartin. But it equally disrupts the novelist's project, the aim of which is to substitute the grand table of social species in mutation for the private distresses of chatelain souls. At this point, indeed, the disorder of social conditions joins the pictorial revolution to define a form of plot that works discreetly but surely to undercut any attempt to compile a novelistic summa identical to this table of social species. For the caricature of Esgrignon's salon hides a deeper problem, one that Balzac only half-formulates in his preface to *A Daughter of Eve*. The table of species was in fact more apposite to the former society. In the latter, everyone was in their place and each individual bore the physiognomy of their social condition: 'social natures were sharply contrasted: a bourgeois was a merchant or an artisan, a nobleman was entirely free, a peasant was a slave. That was European society as it used to be.'[5] But precisely this binding of individuals to a fixed social condition 'lent little to the conditions of the novel'. What did lend to them, on the other hand, was this erasure of differences, this equality whose disastrous consequences for social unity Balzac the ideologue additionally deplored. His reasoning seems, then, to refute in advance Pontmartin's analysis of the decadence of the novel in democratic times. 'Equality is producing infinite nuances in France. In times past, caste gave everyone a physiognomy that took precedence over the individual. Nowadays, the individual's physiognomy is entirely up to himself.'[6] This privilege of the individual would have come at little cost had it not coincided with a small revolution in painting, or rather in pictorial visibility. The times of fixed social types were times of well-delineated forms. The time of individuals and their 'infinite nuances' is one of constant light variations depending upon the hour of day; one of halftones and shadows, of the light vapours that shroud a morning and the chiaroscuros that depict fantastical landscapes at the close of day; a time when the artist's eye dwells on the bizarre hieroglyphs formed by the beams of old houses, on the flowers bedecking crooked windows and on the young virgins' faces that happen to be framed in them, while the young virgins themselves, dreamy behind their windows like figures in Dutch paintings, read their destinies in 'an unexpected spectacle, the appearance of a place, in something read, in the glance of religious pomp, in a concert of natural scents, in a delightful morning veiled in its fine mists, in some divine music with caressing notes, in a word in some unexpected movement within the soul or within the body'.[7]

So it is that, in the interstices of the great monument that ought to have represented society to itself, new plots are woven, plots born of a circumstance, a reflection of light, a nuance of feeling, a chance framing that iconizes a figure. This complex play unfolds between three gazes:

that of science at a social species, that of art at a genre painting, and that of narration at a fictional love object. It is because the proprietor of the *Cat and Racket* turns out the store lights, in a bid to economize, that the outside gaze breaks in – like in paintings of interiors by Pieter de Hooch, or by his modern imitator, Martin Drolling – and can fix upon the lit background on which, in the eyes of the randomly passing artist, a picture stands out 'that would have arrested every painter in the world':[8] the image of the family's calm bliss while dining under an astral lamp, the brightness of which makes the pensive figure of the young Augustine shine out among the dining room's white linen, silverware and crystalware. Accordingly, the art of fiction is deployed on two planes: crossing from the first plane, on which social species are put on scientific display, it reaches the background, in which pictorial art presents otherwise the upheavals of the social world simply by having an unprecedented plebeian happiness gleam on the faces of shopkeepers' or artisans' daughters.

This very happiness, of course, promises only misfortune to the passer-by who wants to take the woman worker out from behind her window, or to the young woman who permits herself to be turned into the subject of a painting and an object of love. Fiction, it is true, thrives on misfortune in the love relationship. The error by which a genre painting is transformed into a love object is therefore apt to ensure the love relationship rosy days ahead. But things are more serious for fiction itself. The happiness of the pictorial gaze tends to force out the happiness of fictional events, rendering the latter superfluous or artificial. The peculiarities of an ancient façade, the bends of a picturesque street, the light in the late afternoon – all first seem to introduce us into an afternoon directly *in medias res*, right into the time and space of action. In reality, however, they do totally the opposite: they defer this time and space of action by holding us in the contemplation of a past, a moment of suspense or 'the mass of enjoyments floating, at all hours', between the streets' walls.[9] The picture that ought to provide all the elements necessary to getting the action underway tends to confine itself in the time of a suspended reverie, constraining this action to founder on the immobility of its suspended time or feed on the artifice of invented accidents: the fortunes of long-distance navigating or of stock-exchange specu-lation; the misappropriating of wills; the intrigues of the powerful or the facetiae of journalists; bankruptcies or assassinations. This demonstration is offered *in nucleo* by the trivial incident that, in the short tale 'The Purse', literally causes the hero to fall from the infinity of reverie into the peripeteia of fictional action. The tale indeed begins with a long meditation on the moment 'when night has not yet come and day is no longer', when 'the twilight gleam then throws its soft hues or strange reflections on every object, and fosters a reverie that vaguely weds itself to the play of light and shadow'.[10] The dreamer, as it happens, is the young painter Hippolyte Schinner, who is perched on a ladder in front of the painting he is currently working on, but above all absorbed in his enjoyment of the chiaroscuro and the meditations it engenders, lost in that moment when the painter's activity withdraws into the indistinct reverie that gives it its sensible fabric. To bring this suspension to an end and get the action underway, it is necessary to have a simple misstep in the half-light throw the painter to the bottom of the ladder. This fall provides the occasion for the tenant from the floor below to come in and enables, around a story of an embroidered purse, a brief romance to spark that will wind up in a marriage proposal. The action springs, as if reluctantly, from the accident that interrupts the suspension arising from a reverie. And it is ever tempted to return there. The austere investigation of the scholar peering down at the tableau of society, and of the artist wanting to capture on his canvas the light variations colouring an interior or nuancing a facial expression, can, at a pinch, dissolve into the drifting gaze of the daydreamer. Thus, in an episode of *The Wild Ass's Skin*, Raphaël, aloft in his austere scholar's attic, gazes driftingly over the motionless waves of slate and tile roofs that cover 'populous abysses',[11] and catches a glimpse behind this or that window of the profile of an old woman watering nasturtiums or of a young girl's forehead and long locks at her toilette. For behind each window lies the virtuality of a tale, one certainly more credible and perhaps richer in intensity than the extravagant story of the oriental talisman. In this way, by a sort of cinematographic projection, the gaze from dormer to dormer is established in its lengthy proximity to that of the social naturalist. But more happens here: this gaze contaminates the latter with its indifferent curiosity or with its indifferent indifference. The 'human comedy' might have wanted its principle to be that of social science, in which each situation and each action takes on meaning by being articulated with all the others. Ultimately, however, it is that of the window behind which things make sense only by being isolated in the closure of a tableau, and form a tableau only by melting into an indistinct day, by being kept at the ocean's edge where all meaning sinks into the motionless and ever recommenced movement of the waves.

A new sort of equilibrium is thus established between the four terms of the fictional square defined by Aristotle: happiness and misfortune, ignorance and knowledge. The scholar's concern to deduce fictional misfortunes from the knowledge of their social causes is transformed into the painter's happiness, the other side of which is the misfortune of a love that will never abolish the distance between one window and another. This misfortune, in turn, is erased in the happiness of the reverie that embraces, beyond any particular window, the motionless movement of waves and of 'populous abysses'. This happiness is a new sort of knowledge that names no cause and promises no effect. The science of the scholar, with its knowledge of the chain of causation, and that of the dramatist, involved in producing and maintaining the fear of effects, sink together into the abyss of the dreamy gaze of an artist who has adopted in his own way the pity of the young girl at the window, the affect of sensitive souls by which one can recognize one's fellow creature in those who suffer and who hope from behind the window, on the other side of the court.

The Eyes of the Poor

At footpath level, the reflections of daydreamers are offered different gazes at different tableaus. To wit, the gazes of the poor out strolling, stilled by the new enchantments of the boulevard café, which lavishes mythological mirrors, golds and decors on the eyes of passers-by. The customer seated at one, if they are a poet, has an occasion to meditate on what is and is not shared of what eyes see from each side of the glass partitions. This is indeed the new treasure offered to poetry when the windows that had sheltered the torments of elite souls open and the street offers the wealthy and the poor alike the spectacle of others' enjoyment. The poet can now slip into the personage of each passer-by and give himself entirely to 'the unexpected's showing itself'.[12] He thus strives to imagine the thoughts that pass across the eyes of the father admiringly beholding this work of art, of the young child simply dazed by the profusion of light, and of his elder brother, to whom this luxury throws back the image of his exclusion. However, the glimmer in the eyes of poor people standing on the other side of the window is a pleasure that one companion cannot share, her contentment spoilt by those eyes 'as wide open as portes-cochères'.[13]

The metaphor merits our dwelling on it. Perhaps this egotistical fool, whom the wide-eyed poor disturb from savouring her drink, does actually see the disquieting depth hidden behind these foreign glimmers of thought, which the daydreamer thinks he can straightforwardly appropriate. The portes-cochères do not simply metaphorize the stupefaction or the envy of the underprivileged at the splendour of inaccessible luxury. They also signify, for those who taste this luxury, an access, opened an instant and promptly shut, to the depths usually hidden behind them: the unsuspected depths of feeling and affect by which the children of the poor blur the division of sensations and emotions specific to each social condition.

To understand the risk here, we must compare two stories of little girls. Everyone knows the story of Cosette and her dumbstruck look before 'the lady', the giant plush doll that turns the Christmas market stall at Montfermeil into a fabulous palace. The young girl, we know, will not be left dreaming for long about this inaccessible marvel. Pity for the underprivileged indeed arrives, incarnated in the character of Jean Valjean, who also has the means to offer her this luxury. So Cosette will get her doll. And, truth be told, she will have all she wishes to have throughout the whole story. But the price she pays for this is to be herself no more than a doll, one of those 'mannequins' that outraged Flaubert, those 'cloying guys' that one never sees 'suffer in the depth of their soul'.[14] Flaubert's critique here nevertheless contains a small injustice: there is one character in *Les Misérables* in whom the author of *Madame Bovary* might have recognized a sister of the little Justin that he portrays, in faint outline, as Emma's bashful lover; a character in whom – no more than the apprentice pharmacist – we see no depth of soul but whose discreet suffering sings its continuous melody in counterpoint to Cosette's stupid happiness: the street child, Éponine, whom the poet has die on the barricade, all the while granting her the final happiness of being able to profess, in a classical litotes, her poor person's feelings to the one whose life she has just saved, feelings that all the characters are unaware of but that the reader has already long enjoyed having recognized: 'And then, you see, Monsieur Marius, I think I was a little bit in love with you.'[15]

Signalled here, albeit modestly, is the depth hidden behind the portes-cochères, that will not be taken by surprise in any gaze, but that comes to be condensed in an epigram. This condensation itself is worthy of attention. Indeed, a figure of language may often encapsulate a form of fiction and a regime of fictional affect. Aristotelian tragedy, with its chain of causation in which effects are produced contrary to those expected, was homologous to the structure of the bon mot, which inverts the end anticipated at the beginning of the expression and thereby allows the hearer to enjoy their very mistake.[16] This structure of wrong-footing expectation established a play of affects between the fear that anticipates misfortune and the pity that aims at its effects. The litotes in which Éponine's destiny is encapsulated, at the end of a chapter in a work containing over 350 of them, attests to a new economy of the story. The narrative structure leading heroes from one fortune to the opposite fortune is here at once completed and countered by these sidesteps and gazes over the abyss that opens onto a universe of more secret misfortunes, which themselves stand, as though in reserve of fiction, on the boundary separating things that are worthy of being recounted from those which are not. Serving to do this are the chapter endings that take the form of epigrams or of silent scenes that run, between chapters, the thread of a latent narration: the narrating of misfortunes that amount to too little to be told, but that would also lose, if one wanted to recount them in detail, the power that they justly hold to express this world of events and emotions, which offers fiction no subject matter at all. This thread has Éponine run from the moment she enters Marius's room, in which, in addition to the duty her father has ordered (glean, as a pauperess, a bit of money from the neighbour), Marius asks of her a favour (to use her street-kid resourcefulness to find Cosette's address): two acts of service that indicate to her *a contrario* the two roles that history forbids her – to be a wife and to be an object of love.

True, these furtive openings of the tale onto that with which it cannot be burdened contain the germ of a new mode of narration: the short form of the novel or the prose poem. More aptly than the *roman-fleuve* of misery, this form turns the simple misfortune of a life that is nothing into a whole. But to this end it must condense the linkages of a tale into the instantaneousness of a gaze at a furtive scene or of a short story encapsulating an entire life's drama. This story mode tallies best with the broadened affect of pity that structures an attentiveness to events concerning encounters between separate worlds. The broadening of affect has its correlate in a restriction of fictional time and space. It finds its privileged site in these small epigrammatic forms that say everything in the space of a single scene or seek simply to extend its simple resonance.

Cosette's gaze at the prodigious doll, which needs only to be bought at its price, must thus be contrasted with the gaze of another pauperess, by which we may glimpse what vertiginous depths are buried behind those 'portes-cochères'. A short story by Maupassant, *The Chair-Mender*, leaps right into this vertigo.[17] The story is told at a chateau party one evening during which the guests are weighing up whether a single love may fulfil a whole life. The narrator is, as often occurs in Maupassant, a doctor, a man whose profession obliges him to cross between separate worlds and to see suffering that is normally hidden from men and women of his status: not simply the effects of work and extreme poverty on the bodies of the poor but also the effects in their souls of passions that 'proper and respectable people' cannot even imagine them capable of. A poor chair-mender, who had just died, had harboured just such a love for a pharmacist, whose satisfied bourgeois mien his shop window flaunted. This love of a lifetime itself obeys the structure of the epigram. Indeed, it is the extension of a single moment, a moment of madness in which, between the rich and the poor, the happy and the unhappy, the entire natural order of feelings and conducts is cast upside down. The small chair-mender, a daughter of itinerant chair-menders who at that time passed through the town once each year, one fine day stumbled across a spectacle opposite to that exhibited to the boulevard idlers in Baudelaire: the spectacle, simply incomprehensible to her, of wealthy people's unhappiness, epitomized by the tears of that nicely dressed and ever so cute little boy from whom classmates had stolen two *liards*. At this moment she has the unheard-of audacity to take the inversion of roles to the very end: unable to bear the stain that the tears of this happiness-bound being had made on the landscape of the visible, she gives him all seven of the pennies she owns. But she also proves bolder than Éponine, who vainly left it to Marius to guess what her reward was for finding the address before begging him, after having saved his life, for the sole mercy of a posthumous kiss. In effect, the young chair-mender rewards herself forthwith by madly kissing the small boy, who is too consumed with counting the pennies to care. And every year she again inverts the world order for an instant by paying the few pennies she has gathered in the previous twelve months for the kisses she gives to the young, rich boy.

As the high school years and adult life roll around, this idyll ends, and the adored kid turns into a potbellied and honourably married pharmacist who no longer even recognizes his former lover and in exchange for her pennies gives her only medicaments across the counter. The chair-mender's sole resource then consists in saving coins that are not to be exchanged but rather left in inheritance to the honest bourgeois. This confrère of Homais will experience only horror in learning from the doctor, at the same time as about the bequest, of this love that has silently followed him all his life. And he will very logically see it as a disturbance to the public order and a matter for the police: 'Oh If I had known about it while she was alive, I would have had her arrested and bundled off to prison. And she wouldn't have come out again, I can tell you!'[18] But, though he does not want the beggar's love, not even in the past, he needs little persuasion to accept the 2,300 francs of her savings, and thus cements the seductress's triumph despite himself. 'Truly, only women know how to love', the marquise will conclude, as the privileged listener to these stories of impossible love.[19] But this moral, which points to male egotism, conceals another, of which the marquise cannot conceive: only the poor know how to love, how to love beautifully, that is to say, without hope. Without even the hope of filling up more than a few pages of a novella. For it is this very thing that the beauty of the novella is made of.

What Voyeurs See

We know the role that scenes of voyeurism play in *In Search of Lost Time*. Crouching behind a window, the narrator has us share first in the pleasures of Mlle Vinteuil with her musician friend at Montjouvain, then in the encounter between Charlus and Jupien in the court of the Hôtel de Guermantes, and lastly in the sado-masochistic ritual to which the former submits in the brothel of the latter. The relationship between window and sexuality here is easily emphasized. Even without resorting to the Freudian window of the wolf man, we need only recall that the scene at Montjouvain follows the evocation of the young boy's secret pleasures before the open window of the lavatory smelling the iris, and that the young man sets himself at a window overlooking the hotel courtyard to witness a bumblebee pollinating a flower. But the important thing is not to discover, behind the desire to know, the joys and woes of sex. There is more interest in taking things the other way around. Behind Freud's Oedipus lies Aristotle's Oedipus, a character of the theatre par excellence insofar as he is the exemplary witness of the coincidence between the recognition which unveils the unknown *and* the peripeteia that, fating the happy man to unhappiness, inverts the course of the action. Whatever the weight here of the sexual fantasies of Marcel Proust the writer, the *Search*'s voyeuristic scenes are above all paradigms of fictional action as a plot of knowledge. The *Search* is for Proust a novel of knowledge. Now, with Proust, knowledge is acquired in two contradictory and complementary ways: as the fruit of an experience which dispels misleading appearances; and as a revelation that chance alone provides to someone who did not expect it, someone who was not searching to know.

Indeed, this is the supporting paradox of the *Search* and it has a most profound impact on the classical fictional conjunction between knowledge and misfortune. What the narrator needs to know, what he seeks by all available means to discover – the truth about Albertine's 'tastes' – is something of which he will never have any direct revelation. The jealous person can always work himself into the ground watching for and interpreting signs, but this will only ever reinforce the thing that constitutes the essence of jealousy: doubt as to the consequences to be drawn from what has been seen and heard. Signs only ever teach us their insurmountable distance from what they are supposed to reveal. Bodies must be caught in the act. Chance allows for this. But it does so only for one who expects nothing from it. The young man, wearied by his walk and by the heat of summer, dozes off and awakens under a bush that just happens to be right under Mlle Vinteuil's window as the young woman is expecting her lover. The narrator's thirst leads him, not to the cafés in which it might have been quenched had they not been forced to close due to the curfew, but to Jupien's hotel, where Charlus is having himself whipped by nice soldiers on leave pretending to be *apaches de Belleville*. Bodies only confess if one asks nothing of them, if, without wanting it, one catches them red-handed in pleasure. But if this knowledge is unexpectedly offered without corresponding to the subject's desire, nevertheless its discovery must arouse an interest in this subject. How are we to define this interest? The narrator, as character, tells us that this episode has advanced his knowledge of sado-masochism. Yet he is no doctor; he is simply an idler with vain dreams of writing. Thus it is to someone else that this matter is of interest, that is to the writer, who has passed over to the other side and is writing the novel about the narrator's access to knowledge. It is for him that the knowledge gained about the sexuality of a character is of interest. But this interest can clearly not be to learn a truth of which he was unaware. By definition, he knows everything about his characters. His interest lies in showing his readers that his book is a work of science and, in view of this, in contriving their ignorance as well as his character's.

Such is the difficulty of writing a novel of knowledge in the modern age of science. Sophocles' hero needed only to be unaware of the turn taken by the malediction weighing on him. Spectators in Sophocles' time were probably well acquainted with the story of the Labdacid. Yet their appreciation would only have been heightened by seeing the dramatist's skill in arranging the knot between the knowledge acquired by Oedipus and the catastrophe awaiting him. However, the same does not apply in the case of the nameless hero of the *Search*. His era – even if it knew new 'accursed races' – no longer believes in divine malediction and firmly holds that knowledge is beneficial for whomever acquires it. But if it thinks this, it is because knowledge is now the means of escaping a normal condition defined as a condition of ignorance. The narrator's error has to be the error of all those who see what one ordinarily sees: the surface of things. The hero of the coming-of-age novel must therefore not only fill in the gaps in his knowledge and rid himself of youthful illusions. He must set himself down to the exemplary task of overthrowing appearances. He cannot merely be offered the truth from behind a window as though it filled a gap. It must come to him as the contrary of what he believes, as the entry into a world in which the appearances that make up the ordinary landscape of his universe are overthrown. Charlus's being homosexual is not the important thing. It is that this chanced-upon truth is unknown by anyone and even runs exactly counter

to the character that, from the start of the book, all
the others have seen and have us see in him: a virility-
obsessed ladies' man and conspicuous lover of Madame
Swann. What one learns behind the window has a truth
value only as the denunciation of a lie that had taken
everyone in. Thus, both paths of knowledge coincide:
revelation due to chance and the dispelling of appearances. Appearances never dispel themselves and the
science of signs is powerless against deliberate untruth.
At most, it permits of identifying the social species in
a salon. Yet these species are further distinguishable
by their way of lying, such as the 'princess' identified
by her feigned solicitude for people who are not of her
world and with whom she has nothing to do.[20] To know
what a body desires, we must have a naked revelation
of it. But, if this is so, the novelist's science lies not
in the production of knowledge, which requires only
the chance of a presence behind a window. It lies in
producing the deliberate untruth that delays knowledge
so that its secret discovery will be prized all the more.
For that matter, the pleasure of writing shares this with
sexual pleasure. Both of them need untruth: they need
its staging. Proust takes great delight – not without
some naivety – in the idea of inducing the reader into
error on the subject of Charlus. The latter, for his part,
needs to believe that the nice young men that Jupien is
paying to fuel his pleasures are assassins in the making
and enjoy making him suffer. And Mlle Vinteuil needs
to seek 'as far away from her true moral nature as she
could' to find the language which 'her scrupulous and
sensitive heart' knows nothing of, a language befitting
the 'depraved young woman' she desires to be, both to
excite her girlfriend's desire and to succeed in fulfilling
her own.[21]

Here is perhaps where the most radical paradox of
the search for the true is encountered. This paradox

can be formulated first as a simple question: how can the narrator, who has scarcely seen Mlle Vinteuil, except with her father after Mass when they were both children, know so much about her 'true moral nature'? How can he, from the bush under which he must remain lying still to avoid being seen by the woman who is only 'a few centimetres' away, not only see all the gestures and attitudes of the two women and even their winks, but also understand all the intentions behind Mlle Vinteuil's staging and, better still, witness the drama playing out in the bottom of this soul in which 'a timid and supplicant virgin entreated and forced back a rough and swaggering brawler'?[22] If he can, it is because the truth so suddenly revealed to his eyes has the predictable traits of the inverted appearance. Behind the same window quite some time before, the narrator had seen Monsieur Vinteuil play the same game with a score allegedly placed on his piano by mistake as the one that his daughter plays with the supposedly 'misplaced' portrait of her father. He knows that the vicious young girl has a scrupulous and sensitive nature, in the way that the writer Marcel Proust knows that the useless piano teacher is a great composer, that the anti-snob Legrandin is a frustrated snob, that the neighbour, Swann, whom one does not deign to invite around, is a close friend of princes and duchesses, and that Charlus the ladies' man is a homosexual. For the truth to come out, the surprise at the window is necessary, but it is, in itself, nothing other than the inverted appearance. Behind the window the novelist occasionally divulges to the character whose voice he shares a bit of this truth which is but the lie of appearances inverted, but inverted only in the form of a one-off revelation made to a chosen individual. Proust's windows reveal the true only by making it doubly indissociable from untruth: indissociable from the misleading appearance that they happen to belie but also from the misleading staging in which the hidden truth of characters is revealed. The gaze bearing through windows at the truth of bodies' pleasure comes up against the same constraint as the gaze that deciphers the distinguishing signs of social species in salons. The truth of bare bodies seized in their hideaways exists no more than that of dressed bodies observed in society. The truth offered through the window is still one of untruth.

The *Search*'s windows are thus the exact opposite of those through which Stendhal's sincere souls recognize each other at a single glance amid court intrigues and between jail walls. Between these two windows the century of science has passed. This science taught us that there was no such thing as a sincere soul, for the simple reason that no soul knows the truth about itself. It also taught us to recognize the true by a distinctive sign: the true is the exact contrary of that which appears. It has long been known, no doubt, that the habit does not make the monk and that displays of virtue may mask vice. One could observe this merely by consenting, like Orgon, to hide under a table. The observer behind the window at Montjouvain discovers something far more troubling: the vice that goes as the hidden truth of flaunted virtue is itself a parade, an untruth in which virtue is dissimulated. The conclusion draws itself: even in the most privileged situation, the only truth to which sight gives access is that of untruth. The century of Schopenhauer and Ibsen called this the untruth of life and readily saw literature as duty-bound to reveal it. Proust, for his part, believes that a true life exists whose name is literature. But this truth without untruth can only manifest itself in its radical distance from that which is offered to sight. With Plato, one might go from the love of beautiful bodies, of beautiful forms and of beautiful discourses to the love of the Beautiful in itself. With Proust's radical Platonism, this path is closed. The sensible truth, the truth that gives to writing at once its impetus and the text to be deciphered, is manifest only where there is nothing to be seen and nothing to be interpreted: the sound of a hammer or a fork, the creasing of a starched serviette, the taste of a viennoiserie or contact with a loose cobblestone. It is tactile, gustatory or sonorous, always mute, never visual. In relation to its time, then, the Proustian novel of knowledge might well find itself in an analogous position to the Stendhalian novel of sensitive souls. Stendhal inscribed in the world of post-revolutionary plots the encounter of sensitive souls of which the Enlightenment era had dreamt. Proust writes a work of the nineteenth century around 1914 – a novel of the century of knowledge that sought to explain appearances rationally and dispel their conjuring tricks at the price of reaching this disturbing conclusion: there is no truth of sensible appearances. There is truth of the sensible only wherever it does not make anything appear, wherever it is only a noise, a shock, a flavour untied from any promise of meaning, a sensation that refers only to another sensation.

Window with a Street View

The expression crops up often in Rilke, whether in his poems, in his letters or in *The Notebooks of Malte Laurids Brigge*. Someone is standing *at the window*. This person is not said to be looking through the window at the countryside, passers-by or the window opposite. He is not depicted as curious or dreamy. Besides, he is more often seen than seeing. He is simply standing at the window or in front of it, possibly with his back turned to it, as if barring access to it or redoubling its barrier. For the window is apparently no longer the opening by which one appropriates a visible world outside. It has again become the boundary separating the inside from that very outside. But it is also a boundary that changes the very nature of their relation. The outside is no longer something whose contours and figures are given to be seen and known. Rather, it is a dark mass, a force seeking to penetrate, an invasive noise, a contact by which bodies are affected. Its sign is that of the unknown and the disquieting.

Initially, however, the window bore not a threat but a promise. One had to learn how to stand at it again by returning one's gaze at indistinct faraway places in which it became lost, to the consideration of near things. Such was the anti-Romantic programme the poet proposed for himself in an emblematic place for the history of the gaze: the Bay of Naples, in which were concentrated romantic dreams of the sky, the sea, love and adventures:

> But why did our forebears read all about these foreign worlds? [...] they stood at the window with a gaze that almost scornfully turned its back upon the court and the garden out there – they quite literally conjured up that which we now have to do and, as it were, to make good. With their surroundings, which they no longer saw, they lost sight of all reality, the near seemed to them boring and commonplace, and what distance was depended upon their mood and imagination. And in the process near and far passed into oblivion.[23]

The task thus first appeared simple: to incline the gaze as it returned from the indefinite horizon toward the circles of near things that it can embrace with accuracy. The poet, however, sees in this more than a drawing nearer: a conversion. The forebears had turned their backs on the courtyard and the garden. Turning anew toward the outside would thus be necessary. But this turn is not simply a reversal by which the near is put in the place of the distant, in the way that critical spirits in the Romantic era had opposed the solid earth to the speculative sky. This movement is one that no longer distinguishes between the near and the distant, that knows that the distant acts on us through the near. The problem is therefore to know what acting on means. The forebears' mistake was not simply to forget the near to the benefit of the distant. It was to believe that the outside could be appropriated, be made one's own. But no place exists in us to which the outside could be added. The outside does not penetrate. It acts on us. And it acts from afar. In times of so-called realist literature, Flaubert thought that the light that shone in his eye had perhaps been taken 'to the hearth of some still unknown planet' and sometimes he felt himself enter into 'a pebble, an animal, a painting' by dint of looking at them.[24] These pantheistic fantasies no longer obtain in the so-called symbolist age. In this age, even the most dis-embodied of poets knows that 'the ring on my hand can no more enter into me than the farthest stars can enter into us'.[25] Things do not reach us only like light rays striking us.

True, a favourable analogy can still be drawn from this. The things that act on these doorless and windowless monads could here play the role of the magnet that, from a distance, arouses and arranges the hidden forces in an object. At this price a vision of poetry can be upheld as a way of living that is at once accompanied by the order of the world and sheltered from its assaults. Poetry thus gets defined as doing work on the history that each person carries within themselves, a work sheltered by the order in the house whose walls and rooms, furniture and drawers a history has also shaped. The use of this model by Malte Laurids Brigge stems from Francis Jammes, a poet who lived nicely sheltered

in his Béarnaise house in which the very windows seem
to turn toward the inside and send it back its own
light, associated as they are with the glass doors of the
bookcase, which 'pensively reflect the solitary, dearly
loved distance'.[26] Such is the poet's house: a room of
mirrors in which the names of young girls from the past
are drawn out in light ribbons across his verses similar
to the way their tufted tulle dresses are drawn out of the
chest of drawers that are supposed to have stored them
in some room that has remained self-same.

However, this evocation stands only as a contrast to
that poet-of-no-house whose old items of furniture are
rotting away in a barn. 'Things turned out differently.'[27]
Here, however, it is not simply a matter of the trials
and tribulations of a poet's life or of the double he has
created for himself. It is a matter of the knowledge that
one now has about life and the windows that separate
beings from the outside world without protecting them
from it. This twofold lesson is one that the playwright
Maeterlinck, also a master-thinker of his time, would
dispense to an entire generation, a lesson encapsulated in a short play for puppet theatre precisely titled
Interior, albeit the entire dialogue takes place outside.
The dialogue indeed remains privy only to the characters
who observe through a window a family that is unable
to see them. This family, gathered around a lamp, is
still unaware of what the speakers on the outside know
but have yet to come and announce by ringing at the
door located on the other side of the house: one of the
family's daughters has thrown herself into a lake and
her body has just been recovered. Far from all transparency, the three windows of the house seem to form
a frontier between two types of powerlessness. Those
who are inside are held in ignorance by the illusory
security of their closed doors and the peaceful light
around which their circle is gathered. The young girls

inside go over to the windows, but do so with eyes that see nothing, because they seek nothing. Those outside, by contrast, see all without being seen. But this privilege only delays the moment at which they will have to say what it is they know. For the vain privilege of their knowledge, the young girl's suicide and the house's illusory quietude are three effects of one and the same cause: there is no harmony between inside and outside. There are neither transparent windows for them to communicate through, nor closed doors holding them at a distance from one another. One does not know how far the soul extends around humans; more, one does not know how far the world reaches toward them, into them. The window of the play – opaque on the inside and uselessly transparent on the outside – embodies that uncertain frontier, in its nature as well as in its effect.

And yet we must always return to the window. Malte sees this lesson embodied in the disposition of another playwright, Ibsen, who remained immobile in his armchair for the last years of his life. Rilke replaces the simple physiological explanation of this withdrawal (the result of a stroke) with another that stems from the very dramaturgy of the inside and the outside. Ibsen indeed seemed to have found the right formula for uniting inside and outside on stage: to make the infinitely small coincide – 'an increase of half a degree in a feeling, [...] the slight cloudiness in a drop of longing; and that infinitesimal change of colour in an atom of trust'[28] – with the most visible phenomena: a fire, a drowning, a fall from a high tower, which is seen from the windows of a family house, and then the avalanche in the upper mountains that concludes his last drama.[29] But this spectacular avalanche may well bury, along with the drama's hero, the very formula for creating dramas itself by coupling the minute variations occurring within souls with the tumult of nature.

The playwright thus sees himself sent back behind the window as to the place where relearning must take place in order to find another formula by observing those men in the street who are themselves the outside. This is how the young poet addresses himself to the mute playwright: 'You wanted to see the passers-by; for the thought had occurred to you that something might be made of them, if once one had resolved to make a start.'[30]

'Resolved to make a start' is not a chance expression. The idea attributed to the immobilized playwright also occupies the mind of the young poet, who, assailed by the noises of the city and the tram's jangling rattle as it passes by the open window of his room located on the fifth floor of a squalid hotel in the Quartier Latin, resides there half-way between the maternity hospital at which poor lives begin and the home at which they draw to a close. It is necessary that he, a perfect nobody, a perfectly insignificant young man, *resolves to make a start*. For he alone seems to have perceived that, by seeking in history books a past that is to be deciphered in itself, by speaking about 'women' or 'children' incognizant that these words have no plural but only an infinity of singulars and that even an individual exists only in a multiplicity of faces, one still clings obstinately to life's surface. For something to happen, someone who has had this strange idea must resolve to make a start, must sit down at their fifth-floor apartment and set down to writing day and night.

But to write means to keep the window open. Malte's problem is not simply that, like his creator, he cannot stand closed rooms with their stuffy air. It is that the sort of writing that sets out to traverse this conventional surface called life demands renouncing the well-protected house that should have been, that *allegedly was*, the poet's house. The author of the

Notebooks of Malte Laurids Brigge will violently reject this house, by confining it within myth and the past. He sets the young Danish poet's childhood within an aristocratic dwelling, peopled with family portraits, chamberlains and countesses, similar to the portraits and the cupboards filled with costumes and dressing-up clothes from former times, the point being to more effectively fix the one who must write in the present of a small room by the window through which he is assailed by the noises of the city.

Here again the issue is not simply a restriction of space. Malte often goes outside, but the city he crosses is itself built like a crumbling house. Attesting to this are the encounters that punctuate his walks. Instead of the dwelling that incorporates and reflects the calm of an age-old history, there is the famous wall – sole vestige of a demolished building – that inspires dread in the walker. The wall is assuredly steeped in the life that has lived within it, but this life, written on its face by the soot of gas pipes and the rust-speckled channel of the toilet plumbing, exhales only its 'stubborn breath', lingering on which is

> the sweat from armpits that makes clothing heavy and the flat reek of mouths and the clammy odour of perspiring feet, the acrid tang of urine and the smell of burning soot, and the steamy greyness of potatoes and the slick, heavy stink of old lard [...] the sweet lingering smell of neglected infants, the whiff of children frightened of going to school and the stuffiness of pubescent boys' beds.[31]

Instead of drawers in secret rooms storing young women's tufted tulle dresses, the young man encounters the enigma of an old beggar who walks the streets lugging around a bedside table, fully exhibiting its only treasures – a few needles and rusty buttons. And the only substitute for the poem's protective ancestral dwelling is ultimately to be found in the small boutiques of antique dealers or print sellers, whose owners read insouciantly, seated behind windows crammed full of articles that nobody buys, and whose back parlours, when lit of an evening, only invite the poet to a dream of motionless existence: 'to buy a full window like that for myself and to sit behind it with a dog for twenty years'.[32]

But one does not write in these back parlours open to the gaze of the passer-by. One only creates a tableau in them, even if Balzac's Dutch genre painting and its virginal figure is transformed with Rilke into a religious tableau celebrating the consecration of the bread and the wine.[33] Writing now demands that one face windows at once more opaque and more open to the threat of the outside, windows symbolizing the very uncertainty of the boundary between inside and outside. Resolving to make a start and write goes hand in hand with another command, which is to learn how to see. And to see implies that one make 'something of the passers-by'. For this to happen, one must expose oneself to the spectacle of the outside. But the problem is not to train one's gaze by attending to the street in its multiplicity and diversity. This temptation is the all-too-simple one offered by the emblematic spectacle of people passing beneath the poet's windows: a woman pushing a small hand-cart loaded with a barrel-organ, a young boy who accompanies the music by stamping about in his cot and a young girl dancing and shaking a tambourine up at the windows. Seen from above, the spectacle of a poor and industrious life simply retains the usual distance and ordinary laziness of the gaze that knows what it sees and what kind of thing it is. Learning to see, by contrast, means learning to subtract the gaze from its ordinary exercise. And to do this, the distance must be eliminated by going into the street and losing oneself in that outside to which 'there is no end',[34] by exposing the gaze to that which permits of no enframing, to that which acts on it, shocks it, intrigues it and that it cannot bear. These are the street spectacles that hamper Malte's urban route: the man with St Vitus's dance who hops along the boulevard Saint-Michel; the man who gives bread to the birds and who stands there 'like a candle burning down, the remainder of the wick still glowing';[35] the blind newspaper seller at the Luxembourg Gardens whose mouth is drawn in, 'like the spout of a drain', whose hand is worn out by the stone coping on which it rests, and the remnants of whose voice are 'no different from a noise from inside a lamp or a stove, or when drops fall at odd intervals in an underground cave'.[36] For whoever allows them to approach, these attacks from the outside have a very precise virtue: they teach one to unlearn. Therein lies the virtue of the real: it obliges one to cease imagining. Ceasing to imagine here does not mean to stop losing oneself in illusory creations. If the imagination prohibits seeing, this is not, as it is said, because it leads the mind to stray far from reality. On the contrary, it is because it gives one possession of reality in advance. To cease to imagine is to cease to hold to the schema whereby one already knows what is presented to one's eyes, a schema preceding and ordering each encounter. But it also means bidding farewell to the new capacity that poetry, with Baudelaire, had arrogated for itself: that of penetrating into the body of every passer-by to become its intimate soul. Malte's perambulations around Paris's streets are the exact opposite, the exact refutation of the poet's holy intoxication as he enjoys entering into the personages of the anonymous crowd.

This is the exemplary lesson dispensed by the old woman with the bedside-table drawer who stands obstinately in front of the window, which the young man feigns to look at so as not to meet her gaze. She stands there 'pushing forth a long, old pencil from out of her sorry, clenched hands'.[37] The scene is not one that Malte's creator made up. It was something he witnessed during his first stay in Paris, and in the presence of this piddling pencil, which seemed to bear all the weight of a destiny, he was overcome with fright. Nevertheless, the wholly prosaic sense of this disturbing gesture ultimately did not escape him: the old woman simply wished to sell him the pencil.[38] But by ascribing the adventure to Malte, he abolishes the denouement and transforms the very meaning of the gesture and the anxiety it produces:

> I affected to be studying the window display and to have noticed nothing. But she knew that I'd seen her, she knew that I was standing and wondering what she was really doing. For I was perfectly aware that it wasn't about the pencil. I sensed that it was a signal, a sign for the initiated, a sign the untouchables recognize. I felt intuitively that she was prompting me to go somewhere or do something.[39]

The sense of the transformation Rilke effectuates is clear: the experience that the old beggar affords is no longer that of misery calling out for help. It is that of a world in which no gesture, even while it signals, bears its meaning in itself. This defection of meaning first suggests the idea that the excluded have a secret language. But it much rather tends to an ultimate defection, which is that of the sensible universe itself. It tends to the moment at which all bearings are lost by which one might take up a place in the universe. This loss is exhibited by the intruder who, in the dairy shop where the poet goes to eat with the poor, is seated at the table that the poet usually sits at and forces on the latter's terror-filled gaze the spectacle of a life in the process of withdrawing: 'One moment more and everything would have lost its meaning, and this table, and the cup and the chair he was clinging to, all the everyday and the near, would have become incomprehensible, alien, difficult.'[40] This loss of meaning and of all meaning, which for the old man signifies impending death, is nevertheless what truly brings the young man closer to the life to come, the life yet unknown but that perhaps shall be one day for those who consent to wrest themselves from dearly held meanings. Corresponding to the hand of the old woman letting that absurd pencil slide between her fingers is, then, the poet's hand as it recedes from him and writes words that he will not have intended, words that will untie and in which each meaning will be deferred and come pelting down in rain.[41] At this point the dream of the protective house gets turned totally inside out. Writing will have its condition in the attack of an outside that teaches us to see by undoing the coherence of every sensible synthesis. This is, paradoxically, what can be done with passers-by: not to observe them from the window but to go down among them, to follow them to the point at which they no longer pass by, at which they become immobile, at which their eyes no longer see, their voices are but the murmur of a lamp, their bodies but the remains of a candle consuming itself – to share the 'little time' separating them from their transformation into inert things.

The poet was made aware of this sharing by another writer, a sharing that falls under the patronage of a saint: the Saint Julien Hospitaller that Flaubert has come down from his stained-glass window to tell his story, one about a Christian Oedipus who flees the paternal household to avoid killing his parents, but who nonetheless kills them by mistake, and, for his expiation, becomes a beggar and winds up sharing his bed with a leper. 'Embrace the leper' is the commanding figure that organizes the procession of beggars and monsters that emerge to greet the poet in the streets of Paris. It is the end that the poet indefinitely approaches without the encounter coming to completion. An image is clearly only an image, so no reader expects the young man actually to embrace a leper. But, as it happens, this image is one of a recent attainment that is bound to remain incomplete. The young poet 'still does offer resistance', where the old man in the dairy shop no longer offers any. He sees death on the face of this dying person but it is while rushing out the door; similarly, he stares fixedly at the hands still containing the hollow mould of a face, and thus avoids, by lifting his eyes, the sight of the flayed head. For, decided as he is to go through the surface and reach yet-unknown true life, he doubts that living is going to be possible again after the metamorphosis which has engulfed the entire familiar sensible universe. He does not give up on the idea that he will indeed find for himself some solitary and protective dwelling, shaped by time and use, in which it will be possible to sit down calmly, back turned to the window, to transcribe the experience of the passer-by who unlearned to ill-see by brushing against every experience of dispossession. 'Standing at the window' also means this: remain in this compromise between two equally absolute and wholly incompatible demands – that of the inside that protects the hand that writes and that of the outside that, taking all protection away from the gaze, teaches one to see.

The Threshold of Science

The Commodity's Secret

'The wealth of those societies in which the capitalist mode of production prevails, presents itself as an "immense collection of commodities"; the individual commodity appears as its elementary form. Our investigation therefore begins with the analysis of the commodity.'[1]

The first two sentences of *Capital* indicate at once the path that the author intends to follow and this path's conformity with the general scientific approach: the latter commands that one set out from the empirical designation of a reality but then immediately take a distance from this reality and submit its terms to questioning. The scientist thus asks what this 'commodity' is, in its essence, insofar as accumulating commodities seems a patently obvious thing to do. But this simple passage from the false empirical self-evidence of the multiple to the theoretical formulation of its essence proves misleading. A promise to analyse a multiple reality is usually a promise to reduce it to its basic elements. Yet, this search is immediately escorted here by its contradiction. Setting out on a search for the basic unit named the commodity means obstinately encountering a duality: object of utility and depository of value, use value and exchange value, concrete labour and abstract labour, relative form and equivalent form, value of work and value of labour power, and so on. But this also means encountering the duplicity of the commodity – which lies about its simplicity – and of commodity exchange – which lies about the simplicity of the twoness constituting it. It means recognizing the dissimulation of the commodity. But it simultaneously means recognizing that this dissimulation is not a lie that one must get inside, that it is the commodity's way of speaking truly about the dissimulation constituting it. The commodity's appearance is not some illusion to get behind in order to discover the truth; it is the phantasmagoria attesting to the truth of a metamorphic process. The scientific exposé is about deploying a theatre of metamorphoses. It is this theatre that must be reconstructed from the simple thingness of a commodity or from the simple exchange of commodities that two individuals undertake. Behind one scene of metamorphoses, there is always another scene taking place. Analysis is not the reduction of the multiple to the simple but the discovery of the duplicity hidden in every simplicity and of the secret of that duplicity, which manifests itself in another theatre where it is at once unveiled and covered over anew. The work of science is not to disenchant a world whose occupants are supposedly lost in illusory representations. It must show, conversely, that the world that sober minds deem prosaic is actually enchanted, whereby its constitutive sorcery must be discovered.

Hence the fact that the demonstration is also a story that plunges into the heart of a secret. Hence, also, the constant deferment of this nonetheless quickly grasped secret. Marx indeed needs only a few pages to unveil the heart of the entire matter. 'Now we know the substance of value. It is labour. We know the measure of its magnitude. It is labour-time.'² From there it would seem one could go straight to the essential point: what is concealed is time. Commodity exchange is the way in which, in capitalism, the impalpable reality of the global distribution of social labour time is translated, a reality that is, in this system, also the reality of stolen time: not simply unpaid work time but the time for living that the victims of exploitation are docked. But this straight path is carefully spiked with barriers that, one by one, must be cleared away so that each time we discover that the task of revelation imposes the longest detour, that each one of the operations in which commodities are engaged is in fact the resolution of a contradiction, that a commodity cannot be exchanged for another unless each of them occupies an opposite, incomparable place. Serving this end is the singular dramaturgy of the encounter between the linen and the coat, from which the analysis of the commodity is developed: 'Let us take two commodities, such as a coat and 10 yards of linen, and let the value of the first be twice the value of the second, so that, if 10 yards of linen = W, the coat = 2W.'³ What exactly is the status of this *example*? Clearly, it is not a matter of some situation borrowed from the empirical reality of exchanges. If it is a matter of showing the capitalist reality of commodity circulation, then this linen seller selling his goods for half a coat is clearly contrary to type. It must thus be seen that this point of departure in fact advances an entirely abstract model of exchange. But, in this case, why be burdened by these pieces of linen? Why not simply use mathematical symbols? It must thus be concluded that this coat and this linen are neither empirical examples nor abstractions clothed for convenience. They are the characters of a play. And it is owing neither to the author's coquetry nor to his concern for fun teaching methods that Marx lends them a language, a gaze, a sentiment, as well as arguments and loving emotions. If they speak and if, on occasion, they use sophisms, if they seek a kindred spirit and desire to enter into the body of the other, it is for two reasons: on the one hand, it is because they thus do something that they *cannot*, and by vainly trying their hand at doing it they confess to being neither real things nor real persons but fantastical beings whose secret of manufacture must be discovered. On the other hand, it is also to occupy the stage in place of the things that would be real things and the persons who would be real persons.

For what is at stake in the analysis is not simply to reveal the historical reality of the capitalist mode of commodity production behind the supposed eternal laws of the economy. Just as much, if not more, it is to prohibit a certain form of critique of the economy and a certain way of resolving its contradictions. Indeed, there is an apparently simpler way of dispelling both the phantasmagoria of market exchange and the relation of exploitation it expresses, a way that suppresses at once the mediations of the dialectic and the intermediaries of property. That the commodity is at once an object that meets a need and the embodiment of an average social labour time does not necessitate seeing a contradiction in it. One may simply see in it a complementarity that is to be harmoniously regulated. Humans trade the objects they need. They also need, for the labour time that they devote to producing objects useful to others, to be remunerated in such a way as to permit them to obtain objects of use to themselves. The condition of this equal exchange is the elimination of the parasite that strives to reduce remuneration for the work done and to increase the price of its product, namely the theft perpetrated on work by property. The producers of wealth need only to recognize that there is neither a mystery nor an evil spell in their products, but simply an equilibrium to be achieved and that can be achieved if they agree to exchange their products among themselves – if they turn the exchange of commodities against gold into an exchange of services among producers. That, in sum, is the simplest way for the reified world of commodities to be rendered unto the human subjects whose powers have been alienated in it.

The Marxist tale of the commodity's enchantments is made, first, to bar this happy ending to the capitalist curse: that republic of free producers dreamed of by the militants of workers' associations and for which Proudhon delivered the theoretical formula. The analysis of the contradictions and sophisms of the sensible-supra-sensible being named the commodity is a war-machine directed less against the economic science of capitalism than against this prosaic liquidation of capitalist exploitation. It is made above all to say: no direct exchange of services and products is able to replace the unequal exchange of commodities. As soon as the global distribution of social work takes the figure of an exchange of products, these products can only be commodities. And 'independent' producers exchange their products freely only insofar as they are dependent on the system of global dependency embodied in these products. Free agreement between producers can only be a sublimation of the real exchange of the commodity 'labour power' for the commodity 'gold', which itself is but the form under which dead labour sucks time and blood from living labour. In the age of the globalization of productive forces, the reconquest of collective power by producers can no longer take the form of an exchange between products and services. That beyond of capitalist exploitation would be a return to before its birth.

But this judgement is not the simple verdict carried by the science of history that shows stagnation to be impossible and returns to earlier times illusory. It is equally the decision that founds a certain idea of science and of the history of which it is the science. What this idea excludes is not simply anachronism; it is bad history, that which gets rid of the enchantments of metamorphoses at a cheap price so as to avoid passing through the crucible of contradiction. It does not choose science against hi/stories, it decides for one (hi)story over another, a tragic hi/story over a comic hi/story. The characteristic of a real tragic story, as we've known since Aristotle, is the exact coincidence between the production of a knowledge-effect (recognition) and the inversion of a situation (the peripeteia). This inversion is not simply the misfortune that befalls the happy man but the misfortune born of his happiness itself, the effect born of a cause that it would seem ought to have produced the opposite effect. Bad tragedy, by contrast, replaces inversion with 'equitable' remuneration, such that the good are recompensed and the bad punished. Yet, this equitable settlement brings tragedy closer to comedy, in which the inversion of situations simply gets turned into a reconciliation of characters: 'It belongs rather to comedy, where the bitterest enemies in the piece (e.g. Orestes and Aegisthus) walk off good friends at the end, with no slaying of any one by any one.'⁴

The Proudhonian cutting out of parasites in favour of a direct agreement between producers is a comedy of this kind. It is the erasure of a productive contradiction in favour of a reconciliation that remunerates each according to their work. What Marx meant to exclude is this conciliation, this becoming friends of enemies. And to exclude it from the denouement, it must be excluded from the very construction of the situation. What must be made impossible from the start is that characters who are enemies can end up friends. Now, precisely this elimination is ensured by the initial dramaturgy of the one-on-one encounter between the linen and the coat. In this dramaturgy 'enmity' is posited from the outset, and it is posited not as accidental but as structural. The way in which each of the characters relates to the other is only ever the way in which one's 'enmity' or one's internal contradiction is expressed. Being at once a useful object and an abstract expression of value, this duality must be an internal contradiction in the piece of linen itself at the same time as being invisible in the threads out of which it is woven. This contradiction can be revealed only in an operation of exchange in which the value of each commodity is distributed in two forms that are 'mutually exclusive or opposed extremes'.[5] Which is to say that this enmity can only be revealed to science by being concealed from the gaze in that pure harmony of kindred spirits, which the analysis must undo before the confrontation of the commodity with the general equivalent of gold reveals the *'salto mortale'* at the core of every simple exchange and the permanent possibility that the commodity's love for money is not repaid.[6]

This process of revealing and covering up the contradiction is formulated only 'in the language of commodities', in their enigmatic language, which only ever says the truth by concealing it. In this, the phantasmagoria of commodities also excludes the comedy of friends. If the characters cannot become friends at the end, the simple and sufficient reason is that they are not characters. It is not the producers or traders of commodities who speak and act in this dramaturgy. It is the commodities themselves. And they do so, of course, in their own way – that of 'sensible-suprasensible' beings. The sensible-suprasensible being is a being whose mode of manifestation reveals that its form is the product of a metamorphosis, that it results from a process that takes place on another scene. Its mode of being is that of a hybrid: a phantom that is lent thought, voice, sight, feeling or action only so as to demonstrate that its scene of effectivity is not that of real personages; an automaton whose movements indicate that the energies animating them come from elsewhere, that is, from a 'social relationship' which is exactly not the one that a commodity's buyer and seller entertain. Namely, a social relationship that is the automatism of a global system of dependency, one in which an 'enmity' always reveals a more fundamental 'enmity', in which revelation always refers to a deeper secret, and in which even the recognition of the automaton's secret is not enough to reverse its effect.

For the revealed secret here is a double matter: science works to untangle the enigma into which it transformed the apparently clear-cut formula of commodity exchange. But this work of revelation also proceeds in another manner at the very heart of empirical reality. The change of theoretical terrain that science requires so as to dispel the misleading appearance seen at first glance is indeed coupled with another shift: one toward an empirical place where the truth disguised in these appearances is also given 'at first glance'. This splitting exemplarily illustrates the view solemnly imparted to the reader as a farewell is bid to these exchangers of linen and coats and capital is inspected at the point at which it purports to buy at its price the commodity it calls labour:

> Let us therefore, in company with the owner of money and the owner of labour power, leave this noisy sphere, where everything takes place on the surface and in full view of everyone, and follow them into the hidden abode of production, on whose threshold there hangs a notice 'No admittance except on business'. Here we shall see, not only how capital produces, but how capital is itself produced. The secret of profit-making must at least be laid bare.[7]

This passing from the noisy site of appearances to the secret laboratory gives a somewhat misleading account of the movement of science. For it was not the 'noisy sphere' of exchanges that filled the preceding pages. It was a dramaturgy that transformed this calm surface into a fantastical tale of phantoms and automatons and thus anticipated the voyage into the heart of the process of metamorphoses: the existence of a commodity endowed with the miraculous power to create value – the force of human labour – and of a laboratory devoted to the forced exploitation of this miraculous power. More, however, both this laboratory's localization and the qualification of its secret give way to ambiguity. On the one hand, this laboratory is not a laboratory. The term is a metaphor to indicate the site of science, the work of analysis that will yield the secret's formula: that of the appropriation of surplus labour that is precisely not etched on any place where it could simply be sought out. On the other hand, this laboratory designates a site of real experimentation: Capital's massive experimentation on the bodies of men, women and children in order to produce this surplus labour. Now, this experimentation can be seen at work if one leaves the offices and libraries of the learned to see what is being carried out on production sites everywhere. Worker districts reveal a landscape in which these contradictions can already be seen to be directly materialized, while elsewhere they require analysis to be recognized:

> The intimate connexion between the pangs of hunger suffered by the most industrious layers of the working class, and the extravagant consumption, coarse or refined, of the rich, for which capitalist accumulation is the basis, is only uncovered when the economic laws are known. It is otherwise with the housing situation. Every unprejudiced observer sees that the greater the centralization

of the means of production, the greater is the corresponding concentration of workers within a given space;
and therefore the more quickly capitalist accumulation
takes place, the more miserable the housing situation of
the working class.[8]

If we go through the doors of the factories we will see
that this law of inverse proportion, already visible on
the ground, is the product of a large-scale experiment
on the workers' bodies, an operation that is never said
to be such, but whose actions are at all times visible and
are everywhere confessed in practice by those who are
unaware of it in words.

The prosaic world of the factories is in itself a
vast laboratory, in which experts in extracting unpaid
labour undertake a large-scale experiment *in corpore
vili*. In this laboratory, it is a matter of extracting the
maximum amount of surplus labour that bodies are
able to produce and, to this end, of having perma-
nently at one's disposal the greatest number of workers'
bodies with the property of producing more value than
their production and upkeep costs: bodies to hand at
all times, able to be employed and paid only for the
time that they serve; adult male bodies, when the work
demands particular strength or qualification; women's
and children's bodies, which are less costly, when the
work is easier and demands only that the bodies be
there to carry out the necessary and sufficient acts for
the longest possible time. To this end, the time during
which the worker reproduces simply the value of his
labour power must be reduced to a strict minimum, and
the time in which he produces a new value extended
to a maximum. Short of being able, like Wallachian
boyars, to statutorily transform twelve days of corvée
into fifty-six, it is necessary to upset people's temporal
rhythms and breaks, to reduce meal and sleep times,

to scramble, by means of the relay system, the very difference between day and night, to render unverifiable the names and ages of the children employed, as well as the length of time for which they work. By the same token, the limits set on childhood and adulthood must be loosened. Each of these operations avows the heart of the system: the daily theft not simply of created value, but of the time for living that creates it. This time for living that, each day, is reduced to a time of survival, and where this very surviving is diminished through an attrition of forces, by rarefied air made unbreathable by factory heat, by cramped and overcrowded workshops and dormitories, and by all the ensuing illnesses that are the small change of one basic illness, encapsulated in the law of the vampiric system, namely the law of inverse proportion, whose simple formula must be disclosed behind the equations of exchange: life made short by long hours.

The laboratory's great secret is, in sum, inscribed twice over: once in the scientific operations by which sensible self-evidences are deconstructed to arrive at the formula of inequality hidden in the equations of exchange; and once directly on the bodies whose time for life is sucked dry in the vampire's laboratory. On occasion, this writing of the law of inverse proportion on bodies is laid bare for the attention of public opinion: causing a stir in the press was the case of Mary-Anne Walkley, a young woman who died at twenty years of age in June 1863 after having worked for twenty-six hours non-stop – *saison oblige* – to make outfits for 'Madame Elise' for a Court ball to honour the new Princess of Wales. But this law parades unmasked through all the reports that, duly commissioned by respectable Members of Parliament, were written up by factory doctors and inspectors. These individuals accurately gather the testimonies of nine-year-old children who sleep on a foundry floor before beginning their work day at three in the morning.[9] With their own eyes they see the rooms of twelve square feet in which fifteen to twenty children, 'piled up like herring', work fifteen-hour days with an attention and speed that does not even permit them to raise their eyes for an instant to reply to the investigators' questions.[10] They calculate the cubic content of air granted the women and children of the factories and compare it to what medical science deems necessary. They note that the time-stealing machine cannot be stopped, so that if a child due for a shift is missing, another who has already finished their work day must continue working instead. They note that the bosses make no mystery of it and always end up confessing the grand secret of overexploiting the time for living. Some bosses do so with a certain discomfort: 'Our objections to not allowing boys under 18 to work at night, would be on account of the increase of expense … Skilled hands and the heads in every department are difficult to get, but of lads we could get any number.'[11] Others sum up their 'small thefts' in a frank and limpid formula: 'If you allow me (as I was informed by a highly respectable master) to have workers work only ten minutes in the day over-time, you put one thousand pounds a year in my pocket. Moments are the elements of profit.'[12] These 'confessions', taken from inspectors' blue books, accompany each moment in the analysis of the production process: the simple work day, which produces absolute surplus value; the intensified work day, which produces relative surplus value; the process of capital accumulation, which produces a working class in ever more excessive numbers, ever more crammed into overly small dwellings. They take us right to the revelation of the secret's secret: this primitive accumulation by which workers are expropriated through violence, separates them from their means of living and obliges them, by the enforcing of savage laws, to put their bodies at the disposal of the blood-sucking monster thus produced. This history is not only recorded in manuscripts in which it is described at length. It is 'written in the annals of mankind in letters of blood and fire'.[13]

The secret of surplus value is deciphered with difficulty through science. Time theft and the destruction of lives are everywhere written on bodies. This tension between the hidden and the patent gives to Book One of *Capital* – the only one that Marx published, the only one to which he gave the completed form of a book – its singular narrative structure. This singularity is the conjunction of two movements running in opposite directions. Indeed, the growing complication of the analysis that gives an account of the development of capitalist production goes hand-in-hand with a countermovement that, conversely, ever reduces the complexity of the process to the bare simplicity of the avowed process of extortion and has the end of the book coincide with that process's point of departure, in primitive accumulation's naked acts of violence, which have enabled this complex process to be set up and whose mystery science comes to shed light on: the appropriation of common goods, the violent expropriation of the peasants, laws against vagabonds, the trafficking of sold bodies and the suffering of tortured bodies that created and set in relation the personages of the capitalist scene – accumulated wealth to be exploited and labour power forced to sell itself.

This countermovement is outlined by illustrations that accompany each moment of the process and sometimes seem superfluous. Did so many examples really have to be gathered to illustrate the demonstration of surplus value? Did the testimony of the child potter William Wood really have to be added that of the child J. Murray, then that of the young Fernyhough, which contribute no new element to the analysis?[14] Did match factories and tapestry factories need to be added to the example of potteries, since they depict an identical process, or the picture then completed with an enumeration of the ingredients – human sweat, cobwebs, dead cockroaches, putrid yeast and more – that go into the making of the 'daily bread' sold to the poor?[15] Was it really necessary, in order to refute Malthus and establish the argument of relative overpopulation, to have us visit, subsequent to doctor Hunter, the Richardson house in Wrestlingworth (Bedfordshire), with its plaster walls bulging like a lady's dress in a curtsey and its clay and wood chimney curved like an elephant's trunk and propped up by a long stick;[16] the house of H. in Reenham (Berkshire) with its bedroom without window, fireplace or door, in which a father and his son sleep on the bed in the room while the girls, both of them mothers, sleep in the hall; the bedroom of a house in Tinker's End (Buckinghamshire), in which eight people lived in a room eleven feet long, nine feet broad and six feet five inches high; and a significant number of cottages visited by the same doctor in twelve counties?[17]

Marx gives two reasons to justify this accumulation of examples. The simplest one hints at the boils that prevented his advancing with the 'properly theoretical part' of the book. But his work on this book was not paid by the line. Nothing obliged him to compensate for this delay in the theoretical development by lengthening the 'historical' part. So he adds a second explanation: these 'insertions' constitute a 'supplement' designed to update the book that Engels published in 1845 on *The Condition of the Working Class in England*.[18] The argument itself is flimsy since this supplement is meant above all to show that, in twenty years, nothing has changed. When Engels republishes his book another twenty-five years later, he tends to show, conversely, that things have changed because capitalists no longer need the 'small thefts' that Marx had detailed in his wake.[19] Far more, the book that Marx supplements is his own. But this supplement is something other than an addition. These 'illustrations', which seem to build on each other to corroborate the rigorous scientific tale, in fact compose a second story, the disorder of which obeys another sort of rigour. The point is not simply to use the bruteness of visible facts to refute the expert's sophisms, having already used scientific analyses to refute the false evidences of the visible. Both the theoretical development and the accumulation of examples are subject to a narrative labour. This labour transforms the former into a fantastical tale. It turns the latter into an epic descent into hell. The palpable exchange is turned into a story of phantoms that divulges the hidden contradiction of economic discourse. Conversely, the well-hidden contradiction must be shown to be everywhere exposed, everywhere avowed, as the vampiric, dead labour that, before the eyes of all, feeds daily without let-up on living labour. But the two demonstrations must also be bound together, at the risk of their running in opposite directions. As the contradiction develops and complexifies in the scientific account, the counter-account returns to the fire-and-blood history that is its primary motor, the motor that, for its part, pertains to no science at all.

The nature of the game that science and history play is complicated indeed. Science unveils the contradiction at the heart of the formulae of political economy. And the elaboration of the contradiction must show that its supposed eternal laws are those of a determinate historical mode of production. But how are we to grasp the laws of this mode itself? How are we to grasp their historicity, which is also to say the destruction of the world whose constant reproduction they determine? For this task, more is needed than simply to show that the system's logic is driven by contradiction. The order of the world is made of the harmony of contraries. It is made, as Empedocles had already said, of the very tension between love and hate. And the learned Marx himself agrees. The exchange of commodities can certainly not be carried out unless contradictory conditions are fulfilled. But it is also a contradiction that 'one body constantly falls towards another and at the same time constantly flies away from it'.[20] We might then conceive the movement of capitalist society on the model of the movement of celestial bodies:

> Just as the heavenly bodies always repeat a certain movement, once they have been flung into it, so also does social production, once it has been flung into this movement of alternate expansion and contraction. Effects become causes in their turn, and the various vicissitudes of the whole process, which always reproduces its own conditions, takes on the form of periodicity.[21]

The argument continues and attempts to problematize this normal periodicity by maintaining, by contrast, the possibility and even necessity of shortening cycles and worsening crises. The crux of the problem remains: the normal logic of science is doubly opposed to that of good tragedies, wherein enemy forces become friends and causes produce effects, which in turn become causes that produce the same effects. Where friends become enemies and the effects of causes invert is for another dramaturgy, called history, to deal with.

But this dramaturgy is itself marked by contradictory requirements. On the one hand, history is the process whose mechanism must be revealed behind the so-called natural laws of the economy. This complex mechanism itself has a primary motor. The regularity of commodity movements finds its first cause in the naked violence of primitive accumulation, which gave science its object by leaving in it the mark of its origin – that of fire and blood. This form of historicization, however, which reveals the contingency at the origin of necessity and the 'enmity' at the heart of science, by itself promises no good resolution to the contradiction, no interruption to the regular movement of economic contradictions. The contingency that refutes so-called natural necessity cannot be asked to found another necessity. Primitive accumulation resembles those Shakespearean tragedies in which the murder that gives rise to a reign only ever engenders a new round of murders. To escape this simple matter of sound and fury, the story that countered the necessity of 'nature' had to take it up again on its own account. In this movement, whereby capital is modelled on the revolution of celestial bodies, another prime mover had to be found other than the pure contingency of a history of murder and theft. Now, the solution to the problem does exist. This movement can be set on the soil of another science, that is the new natural history in movement, whose model Cuvier provided in his history of the revolutions of the earthly globe. To do so, we need only marry the geological model of uplifts in the earth's crust with the dialectical model of the negation of negation. Such is the price at which the prime mover's naked violence can be transformed into the statuary midwife of history and at which Shakespearean drama becomes an episode in a natural science of history.

The chapter in which we are shown the regularity of the movement of capital, which came into the world 'dripping from head to toe, from every pore, with blood and dirt',[22] is thus followed by the abrupt appearance, as though fallen from another planet of thought, of another story of the genesis of Capital, in which the latter is rendered as an historical accomplishment of eternal dialectical reason in the form of a geological uplift. The regime of small independent producers who own their means of production cannot, Marx explains, go on forever without 'decreeing universal mediocrity'.[23] This is why,

> At a certain stage of development, [that regime] brings into the world the material means of its own dissolution. From that moment, new forces and new passions spring up in the bosom of society, forces and passions which feel themselves to be fettered by that society. It has to be annihilated; it is annihilated.[24]

Oddly, the preceding chapters had said nothing about these constricted forces and passions, and the end of the same chapter again describes the birth of capitalism as the simple 'expropriation of the mass of the people by a few usurpers'.[25] But this constriction, which comes out of the blue, is necessary insofar as it enables the 'negation of negation' to be identified with a geological process as inevitable as the revolutions of the earthly globe and that guarantees that 'capitalist production begets, with the inexorability of a law of nature, its own negation'.[26] The book can then close by again sealing the breach that determined the very movement of its dramaturgy and leaves to its readers the care of knowing how to use its science to write a new history on the surface of the earth.

Causality's Adventures

According to a learned rumour, the *roman policier* (detective story) was born in April 1841. This was the very month, indeed, that Edgar Allan Poe published 'The Murders in the Rue Morgue' in a New York magazine. What remains to be thought through is the meaning of this birth. Historical and sociological science sometimes view it as an outcome of the era's preoccupation with crime and the situation that it highlights: the dangerousness of those urban spaces with poorly lit, windy streets where criminal networks hide confidently among the flood of new and wretched populations arriving from the countryside or from abroad. In the modern literary tradition, however, what marks the invention of the crime novel genre is something else entirely: a model of fictional rationality that stands opposed to a realist, or psychological, dissolution of novelistic plots. Such is notably how Borges salutes it in the famous preface to *Morel's Invention*.

One fact is easily verifiable: even if the imaginary Rue Morgue – a narrow passage that Poe situates in a populous working-class quarter of Paris – may match the view of crimes as being naturally engendered by the urban breeding ground, the enigmatic murder, whose extraordinary account the narrator and his friend Dupin declaredly read in the evening edition of the *Gazette des tribunaux*, bears scant resemblance to the era-typical crimes and images of criminality that daily filled this newspaper. To see this, we need only read the crime chronicles the *Gazette* reeled off daily and its reports about criminal trials in that same year of 1841. Bar the occasional trap laid at the exit of a popular café for clients having imprudently flaunted their wealth, these matters conform to a dominant model, which is that of family quarrels: misunderstandings between spouses or between parents and children; adulterous, jaded women with violent husbands whom they conspire against with their lover or their daughter or son-in-law; disputes between generations or between parents and parents-in-law over inheritance issues... The result is that, in some neck of the woods or on some riverbank, someone stumbles upon the body, maybe dismembered and disfigured, of a man whose relations, say, had left on business for a few days or had disappeared without informing anyone. The trail leading to the guilty party here is generally easy to trace: the neighbours had already witnessed quarrels and heard threats being uttered; some of them, taken by surprise at these sudden departures, began to gossip; some accomplice let slip a few unfortunate words, so when the investigation was opened, each of the suspects sought to get out of trouble by denouncing the others. The murder is, in short, the final act of an already manifest story of violence. This story unfolds in the family and unravels among neighbours. It is an affair of a proximate nature; its causes never to be sought far away. Accordingly, the shrewdness of police officers is hardly called for to shed light on the crime and identify its author. The only science that intervenes in the matter is the science of doctors, whose minutely detailed autopsy reports make it possible to bring the effect closer to its cause by establishing the probable murder date, the nature of the injuries and the instrument used to strike the fatal blow.

The scene with which the double murder dreamt up by the poet of Baltimore presents us is entirely different. In it, murder assumes the figure of enigma, the solution to which will have to be sought as far as possible from any family or neighbourhood affair. The crime has taken place in a tightly closed-up building and in a room whose door and windows were locked from the inside. The rationality of the fictional police investigation is thus straightaway linked to a certain idea of the place of the crime: a place where entering is as impossible as leaving. And this will also be the case in the era in which reporter Rouletabille seeks to clarify the mystery of the yellow room. The subject of the new genre's crime is inconceivable in its execution. It is also inconceivable in its motivation. Neither the mother nor the daughter were known to have had family feuds. Neither were known to have had other family at all. And the disorder at the crime scene, which usually puts the police on the trail of whoever had been there looking for money, jewellery or papers, conversely deepens the enigma, for one of the elements of this disorder is the presence of two bags lying on the ground containing 4,000 francs in gold that the murderer thumbed his nose at carrying off. The murder and the brutality of its perpetration were motivated by neither interest nor hatred. Truth be told, nothing motivated them. And this consideration, we know, founds Dupin's correct hypothesis: this murder, the execution of which presumed a more-than-human agility and brutality, and the conception of which matched no human interest or sentiment, was not committed by a human being. Confirming this *a contrario* is the only identificatory element contributed by the witnesses: each one of them, whether the Italian or the Spaniard, the Dutchman, the Englishman or the Frenchman, believed he had heard a foreign voice. One might as well say that none of them identified any human voice here. The conclusion draws itself, even if, to verify it, it requires the cunning of a misleading announcement: this double crime is the work of an orangutan. This crime, one might as well say, is not one, since in modern societies it is not standard practice to qualify as such a death inflicted by an animal on a human. Not only does this exemplary crime, whose elucidation symbolically marks the birth of crime fiction, differ from all those with which the justice system and police must usually deal, but, more radically still, it is no crime at all. The new crime genre is born as a paradoxical fictional genre: the elucidation of an event or a series of events in which the specific rationality consists in its radical distance from all the known forms of causal chains of human actions that it might be compared with.

This gap can be conceived in two ways. The first sees in it the occasion to apply mental faculties in excess of the forms of causal rationality ordinarily at stake in human affairs in general and in criminal affairs in particular. What in French is called a *roman policier*, in English is called a *detective story*, and it is indeed born with the character of the detective. Now, this character is not a private or amateur police officer. He is properly a non- or anti-police figure, a man whose social status and mode of thinking are opposed to those of the civil servants dedicated to the ordinary management of crimes and trained in the type of rationality that this management implies. The figure of the detective, which gives the detective story its proper agent, is very exactly an outsider, someone who sees things differently because he stands outside the logics of seeing produced by the social functions of population management and public order maintenance. This outsiderness is the only piece of information that Poe deems useful to provide about his 'detective' Auguste Dupin. Dupin is simply characterized as the son of a well-to-do family who has lost his fortune but nevertheless enjoys a modest rent enabling him to live as he pleases. But living as he pleases for him means living in a way that inverts the normal order of time and the occupations to which it is given. Each morning Dupin says farewell to this order of things by closing his shutters at the first light of day, so that, with his apartment shut tight, he can study by the simple light of candles. Each evening, at nightfall, he steps out to seek, 'amid the wild lights and shadows of the populous city, that infinity of mental excitement which quiet observation can afford'.[27] An imposed darkness during the day, a seeking out of light at night – such are the conditions by which he is able to hone the analytic faculty that stands opposed to the ingenuity of calculating men just as, since Kant, intellectual intuition has stood opposed to the connections of the understanding. The ingenuity of calculating men – professional gamblers, police officers and possibly criminals – is but the mediocre art of ordering, as a series of blows, the causes specific to producing the expected effects. As for the analytic faculty, it is the mental power that matches thought with vision by reuniting in a sole act the ordinarily opposite activities of intuition and deduction. It grasps phenomena diagonally, at mid-distance, whereby a twofold source of errors is avoided: using too small a set of details to make deductions, as this leads sight astray; and losing oneself through thinking in a search for the subterranean causes of phenomena, when everything has rather to be grasped in a single chain on the basis of what is seen. The ideal detective is one who simultaneously opens his eyes wide onto the visible and closes them to order the elements through internal sight.

This form of the relation between outside and inside is the one that makes it possible to untangle the enigma of crimes committed in closed-up spaces into which one cannot enter and from which one cannot leave. And this is again the sort of 'good reasoning' thanks to which, by closing his eyes, the young Rouletabille solves the mystery of the yellow room. The logic of the detective story can indeed not be limited to the simple science of traces passed down from *The Three Princes of Serendip* or Fenimore Cooper's stories of Mohicans. It is not enough to observe traces accurately to identify those who have left them. The relation of traces to their author has to be part of a total chain of causes and effects. And, to see this chain made by closed doors and windows, one has to close one's eyes. The complete interconnectedness of phenomena can be established only in the mind. The faculty of grasping an entire chain of consequences in the unique act of seeing is something that another young man formulated two years prior to the publication of 'The Murders in the Rue Morgue'. This lesson was the one that the young Louis Lambert taught his 'mate' from the college at Vendôme: 'Thinking is seeing [...] Every human science is based on deduction, which is a slow process of seeing by which we work up from the effect to the cause [...].'[28] What one sees must be immediately connected to the chain of thoughts that assign its invisible cause – this mental faculty by which a soul penetrates the secrets of another is paradoxically that one that makes it possible to detect the wholly material 'crime' of an orangutan. This apparent paradox is the simple application of the principle 'the one who can do more, can do less'. Indeed, it was not on account of his acumen for unravelling a police enigma that Dupin had first impressed the narrator, but thanks to his adeptness at accurately reading, while strolling silently alongside him, the narrator's thoughts as they unfolded on his face and in his gestures. This was how Dupin reconstructed the chain by which his companion's thoughts went from the fruiterer whose basket had thrown him to the ground, to a consideration of the unevenness of the cobblestones, to the stereotomy that had been used for the paving stones of another street, to Epicurus' atoms, to the confirmation of atomistic theory by recent cosmogonic discoveries, to the Orion Nebula overhead, and lastly, by means of a Latin verse concerning this constellation, to a satirical article about an ancient cobbler named Chantilly who prided himself on playing tragedy despite his diminutive stature.[29]

The episode is a lesson in philosophy: empirical associations of ideas are merely manifestations of the spiritual interconnectedness of all phenomena. Dupin professes to rule out all supernatural causes from his investigation. But the analytical faculty by which he is able to solve the unsolvable enigma of the double murder distinguishes itself from the calculations of police – and criminals – just as the mind's vision distinguishes itself from fleshly eyesight. Dupin reads the solution in the sight of the disordered room just as he reads the sequence of thoughts on his friend's face. Though Poe's output may not follow the rhythm of French literary actuality, the history of the murders on the rue Morgue arrives right on time between two of Balzac's books: *Louis Lambert*, published two years earlier, and *Ursule Mirouet*, published in feuilleton form the following autumn, and in which the Swedenborgian communication of souls will be key to unmasking the perpetrator of a theft. If detective fiction emerges with Poe, it emerges in a universe of Swedenborgian spirituality, as far as possible from any sociological rationalization of criminality. If it ties literature and science together, this is not, in the first place, via the forms of medical and chemical examination with which police investigation had begun to be associated. As Régis Messac well highlights in his pioneering research, detective fiction emerges as the implementation of a very specific idea of science, embodied by two figures, namely Cuvier and Swedenborg, who simultaneously inspire Balzacian social comedy and its authors' mystical speculations: the scientist who reconstitutes an extinct species on the basis of a single anatomical element and the mystic who inscribes this reconstitution into the universe befitting it – that of the grand connection between beings and events, an entirely spiritual interconnectedness that only a mind with an intelligence endowed with exceptional sensible powers can perceive.[30] The detective novel participates in scientific rationality not by the meticulous studying of clues and laboratory research but by the faithful inscribing of every clue into the chain that emblematized science for a century: that science which, wherever fleshly eyes see only dispersed phenomena, establishes a necessary connection with the whole of the universe. If detective fiction is enduringly connected with 'investigation into a mutilated and dismembered body', it is not to witness the brutality of the crime and its perpetrator, but to offer the analytic faculty the occasion to deploy itself by reinserting this fragment in the great chain of beings. For police and judicial investigation, the dismembered body is that of a victim whose assassin must be found, whereas for the detective endowed with the analytic faculty, it is something completely different: it is an isolated state in a chain of sensible events whose overall articulation must be reconstituted. Some time later, this linking of phenomena in a whole will be identified with a certain idea of materialist science, but for the time being it is thinkable only as an entirely mental linking, accessible only to a deductive capacity identified with the construction of wholly internal, wholly mental senses: that internal world of senses in which the poor Louis Lambert's reason goes to ground but that, more prosaically, enables the ingenuous Ursule Mirouet to come into the possession of her bequest. The crime novel and the philosophical novel are brothers insofar as they communicate within one and the same scientific faith, one and the same idea of science: that which states that there exists, in the universe, an interconnectedness among all phenomena that escapes ordinary intelligence but that can be grasped by the particular form of intelligence able to see the linked in the unlinked.

This is the first way by which the gap between the new crime novel and standard everyday criminality may be thought. This novel is the occasion to wager on a type of rationality that goes beyond normal powers of deduction by perceiving the spiritual interconnectedness among all phenomena. The problem is that this scientific rationality refers to an idea of science that was beginning to flounder at the time. In the 1840s no one any longer expected new discoveries from this idea of science. Which is exactly what made it available for fiction. But this availability only arises through a displacement that unties the complete interconnect-edness of all phenomena from its spiritualist horizon and turns it into a principle of fiction's internal ration-ality. This is therefore the second way in which the gap of detective novel fiction can be thought of and which modernist posterity will salute in Poe. This way does not set itself against the ordinariness of crime and police rationality but against fiction in its realist development. For this, all it needs is to establish a parallel between the method of detective Dupin and the 'philosophy of composition' proclaimed five years earlier by Edgar Allan Poe the poet. This philosophy is demonstrated by the procedure of composition of a poem, but its focal problem is introduced via a supposed ancestor of the detective story, Godwin's *Caleb Williams*. Poe starts by citing Dickens's claim that Godwin developed his novel from its ending, that is from the manhunt, the reason for which is supplied in the later written first part, namely the explanation of the crime committed by a bourgeois above suspicion. Replying to this allegation, Poe puts forward an argument that, after having seduced Baudelaire, will serve as the emblem of a certain idea of literary modernity, that of the unity of effect:

> Nothing is more clear than that every plot, worth the name, must be elaborated to its denouement before anything be attempted with the pen. It is only with the denouement constantly in view that we can give a plot its indispensable air of consequence, or causation, by making the incidents, and especially the tone at all points, tend to the devel-opment of the intention.[31]

In this philosophy, in which some have seen the catchword of literary modernity, one may conversely see a renewed version of the old Aristotelian definition of fictional rationality: the construction of a chain of necessary or verisimilar events that is separated from the chronicle of facts by showing how things *can* occur and all be linked together, instead of simply recounting how they actually transpired, one after the other. Detective fiction led by the 'analytic faculty' offers the exemplary form of a renewed Aristotelianism. If this fiction has to do with modern society, it is negatively. The rationality of making a deduction from instantaneous observation, like that of the unity of effect, endeavours to ward off the danger that this society presents for fictional rationality in the eyes of Poe and those nostalgic for the distinguished universe of belles-lettres alike: the danger that fictional rationality will get bogged down in the universe of prose and its prosaic details.

Here, however, the spiritualist claim of strict causal rationality parts with the nostalgia of reactionaries: the problem is not to dispense with the details but to change their function. True, it might be said that Balzac had already resolved this problem. None of the details with which he overwhelms readers hurrying to see the plot get underway are ancillary to it. Each of them signifies a society and an era. Balzac thus made the furniture of the Maison Grandet speak, as he did the façade of the hôtel du Guénic in *Beatrix* or that of the *The Cat and Racket*. But he could do so on a very precise condition, which was to insert the entomological science of Cuvier into the visionary science of Swedenborg. When this connection is undone, signs return to the state of things, the space of action becomes cluttered and the novelist gets tangled up in it, just like the policemen who, jeered at by Dupin, to find the famous 'stolen letter', examine all the rungs of the chairs and the jointings of all the furniture under the microscope. In the same way, the time of fictional action becomes lost in the details of this or that moment. Novelistic fiction adds something to the fragmented time of the chronicle up until the ultimate identification of action's very motor with the routine of rains and nice weather. Some years later, and in the name of a wholly other idea of science, an unknown novelist would, on the pretext of emending the celestial dreams of his heroine, see no difficulty in likening the progress of a love story – and of the novel recounting it – to the rain that collects on the terraces of houses when the gutters are blocked.[32] This so-called realist novel, with its commonplace characters, its repetitive time and its insignificant events, threatens to drown the ancient logic of fictional action in that 'insipidity and emptiness of each day', whose sway over modern French literature Borges will denounce a century later.[33] By opposing to this literature's greyness the series of marvels that his compatriot, Adolfo Bioy Casares, managed to deduce from a single postulate, Borges well highlights the artificialist tradition that emerges from 'The Murders in the Rue Morgue'. Crime fiction, with its unbelievable events and its extra-lucid geniuses, here appears as a war-machine against the novelty of realism. The so-called unity of action enables it to re-establish a tour de force by which the improbable takes place in logical fashion. Its exemplary function is to order the anarchy of details in which the connections of fictional rationality risked being lost.

But it undertakes to do so at a time when the great dream of the spiritual interconnectedness of everything with everything else is coming undone. This is why, from the outset, the rationality of its plots will be torn between two opposite models. On the one hand, it will wildly raise the stakes of the realist method, in which the detail becomes a sign. On the other, it will reject everything that the eye has presented to it as proof, taking the opposite stance to the one the signs would have us believe. This appears immediately in the conflicting methods used by the *chevalier* Dupin's first two French heirs: namely, the two characters that Émile Gaboriau entrusts with stymieing the ordinary police and judicial logic of the 'ideal culprit' – detective Tabaret and his disciple, the atypical policeman Lecoq.

Hero of *The Lerouge Case*, Tabaret is a scrupulous man in his gathering of traces and clues; he makes the mud outside talk, as he does the dust on the top of wardrobes or the position of the clock's hands. So it is that, at the end of one-and-a-half hours of investigations, he is able to announce to a dumbfounded audience that the Lerouge widow was getting undressed and winding up her cuckoo clock when the assassin, whom she knew well, knocked at the window shutter, this man being still young, of slightly above average height, elegantly dressed, and, who, on that very evening, was wearing a high hat, holding an umbrella and smoking a Trabuco cigar in a holder. The police chief, furious at having the convenient fiction, that of the ideal culprit, jeopardized, is not wrong to denounce in Tabaret a new mode of author who 'has become an amateur detective for the sake of popularity' and who 'professes, with the help of one single fact, to be able to recreate all the details of an assassination, as that savant who from a single bone reconstructed extinct animals'.[34] In any case, Tabaret's performance establishes a genre: in *A Study in Scarlet*, another of Cuvier's and Dupin's disciples, Sherlock Holmes, equally convinced that 'all life is a great chain, the nature of which is known whenever we are shown a single link of it',[35] and capable of divining at a glance the history of a man and his occupation, will dumbfound Doctor Watson and the police in exactly the same manner by announcing to them, after a meticulous examination of the footprints in the mud outside and the dust in the house, that the killer is a man of more than 180 cm in height, has a florid face, remarkably long fingernails on his right hand, was wearing square-toed boots and smoked a Trichinopoly cigar.[36]

The mind certainly feels it more satisfying to use rain to find a murderer's prints in the mud than it does to turn it into the metaphor of provincial love. But these exercises of virtuosity regarding footprints and cigars are still somewhat too prosaic, somewhat too close to the daily mud to be able to illustrate the rationality to which the philosophy of the crime novel is devoted and with which an idea of modern fiction is identified. This is why Lecoq, despite being Tabaret's student, takes a step further when tackling the crime of Orcival. The exhibition of deciphering signs is assuredly apposite to dumbfounding the audience. But dumbfounding one's colleagues is certainly not the problem. The problem is to confound the killer. And the killer, ordinarily, is not an orangutan. It is a human being endowed with intelligence who also understands the logic of signs and can therefore use it to countervailing effect: not to point someone toward the truth but to induce one into error. Anyone in the presence of a profusion of signs must therefore take things the other way around, by thinking that, if these signs are there, visible to the naked, and even trained, eye, it is to carry out the ordinary work of the visible, which is to present appearances apt to conceal the truth, which is by definition invisible. The argument of the uninterrupted continuity of phenomena must then be thwarted by hollowing out anew the gap between appearance and truth. If there are visible signs, it is because they have been arranged to put the investigator off course. The method the investigator will adopt is thus to see them as so many signs that indicate the way in which the crime *did not take place*. This is the lesson Lecoq dispenses. If the corpse was found at the water's edge, then it was placed there deliberately after a murder committed inside the castle. If it is pierced with knife wounds, then the killing was the result of a single blow. If an axe is lying on the floor of the room where the crime probably took place, then the killer did not use it. If the bed is unmade, then no one has been sleeping in it. If there are five glasses on the table, there were not five guests, and for that matter the fact of finding a meal's leftovers on the table is enough to prove that nobody either drank or ate at it.

The Aristotelian rationality of tragic fiction derived from the operation that made the manifestation of truth coincide with the reversal of fortune overwhelming the hero. The new rationality of crime fiction initially appears to renovate and revitalize this logic. But it ultimately leads to something else entirely. Tragic fiction functioned by inverting the meanings of oracles and signs. These latter were veridical. It was simply that the truth proved different from what the hero had believed and what the chain of facts suggested. Lecoq's logic removes this plasticity from signs. It forces them to be either true or false. It thus reduces the mimetic operation of a reversal of appearances – the inversion of what was expected – to the Platonic operation that simply deduces the appearance's falsity from its visibility. The basic criterion that makes the truth the contrary of appearance comes to replace the path leading from a sign to its truth. Police rationality, at a pinch, simply tells us this: the crime was not committed as it appears to have been. In general things do not occur as one thinks they do. The truth is recognized in its being the contrary of what the apparent interconnectedness of phenomena would have us see.

This truth is indeed no longer of the Swedenborg era. It is contemporary, by contrast, with the new figures of the true that accompany the age of positive science: those that, with Schopenhauer, opposed the senseless truth of the will to live to the necessary illusions of the Veil of Maya, or, with Marx, the reality of the process of producing material life and its historical development to the inverted reflections that it produces in the darkroom of ideology. The detective stands opposed to the police functionary just as the scholar who, with Marx, perceives the reality of the economic process from the outside stands opposed to the agent of production, who occupies a position within this process that condemns him to not seeing it. Lecoq's rationality most certainly adheres to these two new modes of scientific faith, as they re-establish, against the simple affirmation of the complete interconnectedness of all phenomena – whereby the issue was merely to see more in a single look – the opposition between the world of visible appearances and that of the invisible truth. This renewed Platonism serves as a theatre for the philosophical and political quarrel over whether the science of the true world makes it possible to change life or whether the lie is that which alone renders this world tolerable. Exactly what this brings to literary fiction still remains to be known – that is, outside of the seductive paradoxes that, in the following century, will play on the confusion between traitor and hero, investigator and criminal or tracker and person tracked. Both the virtuosity enabling one to deduce the type of shoes the killer was wearing and the cigars he smoked, and the wisdom that dismisses too obvious signs, seem incapable of supplying that chain of causation most apposite to distancing fiction from the stagnant waters on the terraces of the realist novel. At a time when shoes and cigars began to be produced and sold en masse, it is already rather fanciful to hope that they could serve to identify a killer. It is even less to be expected that they could furnish the fictional reasoning required: some explanation of the cause-effect links that led this particular individual to commit this specific crime in this place, with or without cigars. The unity of effect – or the linkage of the promised marvels – seems truly to cease at the point where the footprints are correctly matched with the shoes that produced them. It remains entirely bound to the order of efficient causes devoid of final cause. The fine chain of deduction that explains, with a wealth of detail, how the crime was committed does not touch at all on the question of knowing who committed it and why. Dupin dismissed the problem by attributing the double crime of the Rue Morgue to a being that needed no reason to strangle its victims. Yet it was necessary that, close to the victims' house, a Maltese sailor had lived who had had the peculiar idea of setting up in a Parisian apartment with an orangutan. Similarly, Dupin will reckon he's done enough to establish, contrary to the blaze of pernickety refutations published in local newspapers, the exact place and time of Mary Roget's murder, and to prove that it was the deed of a man acting alone, not of a gang. He will have thereby shown once more the necessity for reason to avoid the trap of 'detail'. As for knowing what reason the ghost-like naval officer, identifiable by the periodicity of his appearing and by his way of making a slipknot, might have had for killing that *grisette* in which the reader has no particular reason to be interested, this is manifestly not his problem.

It will most certainly be one for his successors. Knowing the height, and type of high hat and cigars of the Lerouge widow's killer, Tabaret still has no indication that would enable him to trace the matter to the deceitful switching of infants – worthy of *Trouvère* – which is the ultimate reason for the murder. He will have to learn about it quite independently. And this pertains to the realm of pure miracle, since the one who informs him spontaneously of the role played by the Lerouge widow in the baby-switching case is his young neighbour across the landing whom he treats as his own son and who, even more conveniently, will reveal himself to be the killer. Tabaret's science can deduce the killer's height and clothing but, to uncover him, Tabaret already has to have him near at hand, not just as his neighbour across the landing but also as a character from an entirely other sort of fiction, the melodrama of a baby switched at birth. In *A Study in Scarlet*, Sherlock Holmes faces a similar problem: the killer's square-toed boots and Trichinopoly cigars say nothing by themselves about the cause of the murder in an abandoned London house. The cause must stem from elsewhere and even from quite far afield, as with Poe's sailors. And, to explain it, the author must change not only the literary genre, but also the mode of enunciation and ultimately the type of book. Indeed, it is a second book that begins when the novelist divests Watson of speech and gives it to an impersonal narrator who, taking us to Salt Lake City thirty years earlier, tells us the story of the killer, Jefferson Hope, whose fiancée had been snatched and his adoptive father killed by Mormons. If the killer – a righter of wrongs – comes from so far afield, this is because the story of the crime and that of its reasons are two different stories. This original dissociation has accompanied the crime fiction story to this day. Attesting to this in exemplary fashion are Henning Mankell's novels, which, more than once, resolve, deep in the Swedish provinces, affairs of hatred and injustice that originate in the Algerian desert, apartheid South Africa, the plantations of the Caribbean or some other remote theatre of violence. By means of a tour de force they always unite, in one and the same logic, the effects of two kinds of knowledge: one that relates the mutilations suffered by bodies found in a well, a ditch or a lake in a small provincial locality to their causes, and one that relates particular criminal behaviours to the global interconnectedness of political and social relations on a world scale. But this contradiction is not specific to a novelist keen to reconcile his skill as a creator of plots with his political convictions. Global imperialism is neither more nor less out of place in Ystad than the orangutan from Borneo was in the Saint-Roch quarter, the melodrama of the infant switched at birth in a villa of Bougival, or the vengeance wrought by a young man from Nevada on Mormons from Utah in an abandoned house in London. The police rationality that Poe invented sought to oppose the modern novel's lostness in the universe of random beings and things to the beautiful unity of action that reduces every detail to its function and every effect to its causes. But it did so only by splitting action and its rationality. It tightened to the utmost, sometimes to the point of mockery, the chain of efficient causes, but this drove it apart more radically still from the order of final causes. This is why the paradigm that Poe invented served foremost to illustrate to the twentieth century the modernist dogma of literary rationality. For their part, crime fiction authors from the same century knew how to take their distance from it. All refinements concerning the causal plot are banished when another Baltimore native, Dashiell Hammett, strings together the spate of murders in *The Red Harvest*.[37] The cause of the crime is crime itself. It is the existence of a criminal milieu in which the violent settling of scores is normal conduct and becomes the centre of social life through the complicitous actions of moneyed and powerful men. And this milieu, in which criminals, victims and police officers all equally have a hand, is the one that becomes the subject of the crime novel. From Chandler to Ellroy, Hammett's successors have understood that their stories' success would be more assured with the glaucous lights and corruptive atmospheres of the naturalist novel than with the logical paradoxes or the inner seeings of the poet from Baltimore.

The Shores of the Real

The Unimaginable

How does one invent a character? The question seems superfluous. After all, such invention is considered to be the writer's very work. Whoever lacks the imagination necessary to deliver on it, then, would be better off choosing another occupation. This simple demand, it is true, was long escorted by its contrary: what was made up had to be presented as if it hadn't been. This was the function usually played by those stories preceding the story, in which the narrator refuses to acknowledge that the story being related was made up, instead appealing to a chanced-on manuscript, a confided secret or a story heard. This was not, as the sceptics imagine, to have us believe in the objective reality of the events recounted. On the contrary, it was to free the narrator from the concern to guarantee that objective reality. The artifice signalled itself and, by the same token, could be easily forgotten. Readers of the *The Charterhouse of Parma* rarely recall the foreword, which attributes the story to an account of the adventures of Duchesse Sanseverina that the narrator had heard nine years earlier while visiting an old canon friend in Padua. For clearly fiction, with its situations, events and characters, had its own real, quite distinct from the other. One could without contradiction invent and say that one was not inventing.

A time came in the history of fiction when this felicitous conjunction of contraries became impracticable. This is the so-called realist moment. What realism means is not the abdication of the rights of imagination in the face of prosaic reality. It is the loss of bearings that permitted one real to be separated from the other, and therefore also to treat their indistinction as a game. The artifice of inventing and saying that one is not inventing is thus no longer adequate. It becomes a performative contradiction. If a novelist presents this contradiction, it is because the imagination as a faculty of invention has become problematic. This is precisely what seems to be indicated by the strange declaration that abruptly opens Joseph Conrad's novel *Under Western Eyes*: 'To begin with I wish to disclaim the possession of those high gifts of imagination and expression which would have enabled my pen to create for the reader the personality of the man who called himself, after the Russian custom, Cyril son of Isidor – Kirylo Sidorovitch – Razumov.'[1]

Thus speaks the professor of languages, resident in Geneva, charged with the task of recounting the story of Razumov, a St Petersburg student who, after denouncing the perpetrator of a terrorist attack who had confided in him, becomes a double agent, smuggled into revolutionary émigré circles by the Russian police. He would have been unable, he says, to invent the story that he is about to tell. It might be logically concluded that he had no need to invent it, that he is telling it because he witnessed it first-hand. But this is not the case. He has never set foot in Russia. His meetings with Razumov are limited to a few conversations in the streets of Geneva where, what is more, the concerned party proved rather taciturn. And his nature as an honest British citizen prevents him from conceiving of this character's action and motives. It prevents him from understanding these natives of the Russian Empire who can only counter the absolutist repression of all public life with words and dreams of radical destruction. So he must tell the reader how he can tell the story about a personage he barely knew and about whom he can invent nothing. For this he reverts to the old formula of the chanced-on manuscript. But this old formula transforms into the most glaring of contradictions: this Razumov, whom the revolutionaries had chosen as their confidant and whom the police had recruited as a double agent for the same reason – his secretive character – kept a private diary in which he fastidiously recorded the account of his betrayals.

For this unlikelihood, there is, of course, a totally simple explanation. The double agent Razumov is Russian, and the professor of languages, like the novelist, shares the conviction that another writer will sum up later in a lapidary statement: 'The Russians and their disciples have demonstrated, tediously, that no one is impossible.'[2] So there is no need to seek to justify him. But the reader is then inclined to think that the novelist might have been able to avoid turning so laboriously in this circle of unlikelihoods by letting go of his cumbersome professor and entrusting the story to the famous 'omniscient narrator', which itself requires no justification. However, this reasonable conclusion might be a little too simple. On the one hand, the cumbersome professor is there precisely to indicate to readers the radical gap between the conduct of the story's characters and the system of verisimilar reasons that normally establishes support for a story. But, on the other hand, his inability to understand makes him apt to bear the weight of this unimaginable character, a weight of which the novelist, who does not want to deal directly with him, not even as an 'omniscient narrator', is unburdened.

For the all-too-celebrated 'omniscient narrator' in fact encompasses two quite distinct characters. There is the old-style inventor of plots and characters who, retracting from the narration, lets unfold the logical consequences of the situations and characters he has invented. And there is the new narrator dating from Flaubert's era: a narrator who effects the absence of the first person but the respiration of whose sentences marries with the characters' perceptions and affects. This latter narrator is less able than any other to set his characters at a distance. Indeed, this narrator employs another sort of imagination. Conrad formulates its principle tersely in his praise of Maupassant: 'This creative artist has the true imagination; he never condescends to invent anything.'[3] These two clauses suffice to overturn the false idea, endlessly trotted out, about what mimesis means. One who engages in mimesis is not one who reproduces real situations or events by transposing them, but rather one who invents characters and situations that do not exist but that might exist. The true creator does not invent. He does not pull characters out of his head and assign them possible feelings and adventures. On the contrary, he develops the virtualities of stories borne in a really existing sensible state, a sight come upon, a glimpsed form, an unsolicited confidence, an accidently overheard anecdote or one gathered in a book found on the shelf of a second-hand bookstore. That is where the nervous energy must be generated through which the episodes of a story are created if and only if it is first translated into sentences. Flaubert needs to 'have himself see' the scene that he describes. As for Conrad, he assures us that he effectively saw various of his characters pass by in some place or other one day. These characters include Tom Lingard, the Swede from *Victory*, and especially Lord Jim, about whom he wrote the following celebrated lines, which succinctly sum up a whole poetic art, and even a whole regime of art:

> I can safely assure my readers that he [Jim] is not the product of coldly perverted thinking. He's not a figure of the Northern Mists either. One sunny morning, in the commonplace surroundings of an Eastern roadstead, I saw his form pass by – appealing – significant – under a cloud – perfectly silent. Which is as it should be. It was for me, with all the sympathy of which I was capable, to seek fit words for his meaning. He was 'one of us'.[4]

True imagination stands opposed to invented verisimilitude. It is deployed only on the basis of a real kernel: a well cut-out, *characteristic* form in a clear light; an *attractive* form that carries the virtuality of a story; a *silent* form that imposes on the novelist the task of finding the words proper to telling that story. Here only one specific virtue is needed – sympathy. Sympathy is a key notion in Conrad's thought and work, a notion in which an ethics and an aesthetics are intimately united. This notion is doubtless not specific to him. It is consubstantial with modern fiction and it runs through the entire nineteenth century, even changing nature along the way: the pantheistic adherence to the grand unanimous life, illustrated notably by Hugolian poetry, became Schopenhauerian melancholy seeing in pity the most apposite feeling for the will's suffering when pursuing the destructive chimera of its so-called ends. Conradian fiction unfolds against the backdrop of a robust Schopenhauerian nihilism. But, contrary to the dominant version of this nihilism, the novelist draws from it a wholly positive view: the chimera is not an illusion known to a disabused sage. It is the real that sets minds and bodies in movement and that stands opposed to the inventions and rationalizations of verisimilitude. This real is the proper object of the 'imaginative' novelist. His 'imagination' is the construction of a series of 'images', of sense-laden scenes by which characters and situations are extracted from the universe of verisimilitude. But this imaginative power belongs only to those who renounce the position of mastery and submit to the law of a 'feeling-with', if not of a 'suffering-with'. To write the story borne by a form, this approach of imagination and 'sympathy' is very precisely opposed to another, one rather en vogue in Conrad's time, in which one reads on a face the signs of a pathological state. This is the 'scientific' approach of Lombroso or Galton which recognizes in physiognomic features signs indicative of criminality or degeneration. This interest in crime and its indicative signs is foreign to the novelist. What interests the novelist is the chimera, which produces criminals and martyrs alike. This is why, in *Nostromo*, Conrad transforms the rather unedifying story he had heard about a rogue and turns him into a sort of 'romantic mouthpiece of "the people"':[5] the rider of a mare chasing a phantom of glory who answers to the revolutionary chimera of the old Garibaldian, which will ultimately kill him just as the Gould son's industrial chimera did him in, hell-bent as he was on developing the poisoned-gift of a mine he had received. Belonging to the same genre are the chimera of honour that leads Jim to his death, the 'absolutely pure, uncalculating, unpractical spirit of adventure'[6] of Kurtz's Russian disciple, Almayer's absurd business dream and Lingard's vain hopes for his mixed-race daughter. The erstwhile sea adventurer turned sedentary British citizen can imagine all these characters because he had 'met' them one day, because he can sympathize with their chimera, recognizing in it the real of the illusion for which an individual has sacrificed their life. But there is one condition under which this can occur: that this chimera remains their own chimera, the real mirage of a life. Sympathy and imagination together cease wherever the chimera is transformed into a programme that proposes to bring humanity, or such-and-such of its fractions, a happiness founded on reason, science or progress.

Here Conrad's poetics ties to his politics in a mode that at first seems paradoxical. How can the novelist who, in *Heart of Darkness*, described the colonial system's monstrosities more forcefully than any other, display such resolute opposition to the progressive doctrines that fight against the injustices suffered by the wretched of the earth? The reply is simple: these monstrosities are also applications of the doctrine of progress. It was in the name of these words – words learned, recited, recopied outside any reflection – that Kurtz the missionary set out to abolish 'savage customs', that he misjudged the presence deep down inside himself of the 'savagery' he was pretending to combat and that he continued to write his reports to the glory of white man's civilizing mission, all the while accepting to be treated as a god by the indigenous and using their idolatrous faith to assuage what was only a vain fever for ivory. With Kurtz the true lie of the chimera is transformed into a lie pure and simple, into support for the false claim to an historic civilizing mission.

Kurtz still remains imaginable, however, for anyone who has travelled through the Congo, felt the enigma hidden behind the trees lining the shore, glimpsed the whirlwind of black limbs, heard the explosion of cries and beating of feet and hands as though out of the night of the first ages, felt in the civilizers' own stations overwhelming idleness at the same time as the stench in the air of rapine linked to the word 'ivory' and seen those processions of Blacks in chains, being forced to carry materials up steep paths for a railway of no use. This 'anyone' may 'sympathize' with Kurtz because he has experienced, in the encounter with 'savagery', the sentiment of a humanity like our own. Kurtz experienced the affinity between this conquering, western humanity and the night of the first ages. He went to the experiential limit of this human spirit's discovering that it contains all the possibles. His story is, for this reason, far too easily summed up by saying, with the sceptics, that western capitalist man's spirit of rapine is the prosaic truth of the false civilizing mission. For the truth is not the contrary of the chimera; the chimera is the truth itself of experience. And the chimera is the identity of contraries, the spirit of rapine pushing toward the conquest of the earth *and* the only thing that redeems it: 'an idea and an unselfish belief in the idea – something you can set up, and bow down before, and offer a sacrifice to'.[7] Kurtz lived this identity of contraries, but without recognizing it, without being able to express it except via a single word that belies all the humanitarian eloquence of his reports: 'horror'. Because he heard the bewitching call of the banks of the Congo, but also because he knew how, like Marlow, to find some useful maintenance work to resist it and bury 'the thing' threatening to invade the invaders, the novelist can imagine Kurtz; he can write of the confrontation with savagery and the experience of one who has passed over to the other side. He can create 'with all the sympathy of which he is capable' the story of the chimera as stupid rapine *and* as absolute sacrifice to the idea. He can do this because he himself is the son of a defunct chimera (the insurrection of Polish nobles against Russian autocratism) that prohibits him all feelings as regards long durations of time 'outside of fidelity to an absolutely lost cause, to an idea without future'.[8]

The description of colonial horror thus cannot serve any progressive campaign for emancipating the oppressed. On the contrary, it prohibits any synthesis that would place the critique of the lies of progress at the service of true progress. It traces a line of division that renders new fiction possible only by abolishing the possibility of an emancipatory politics. This line separates out two categories of humans: there are those that the novelist can imagine, because he met them or knows the climes that engendered them: those who took the logic of the chimera all the way to the point of it consuming their lives. And there are the others, those he cannot imagine, with whom he cannot sympathize, because he has never met them on the paths along which the flame of the chimera consumes itself. He can only invent these latter, which is also to say, he can only hate them. For the only figure under which he can invent them is precisely that of beings of invention – beings in whom the idea has not taken shape as a chimera and has remained at the state of a dead idea that one manipulates and that manipulates one. Indeed, the dead idea has two major figures: there are words that are merely infinitely manipulable formulae, such as those indefatigably dictated in the comfort of a Geneva villa by the exiled revolutionary in *Under Western Eyes*, or the incendiary words exchanged between anarchists gathered in the secret agent Verloc's London back parlour. And there are plans to organize events to engender stupefaction and fear in those who witness it. This figure of the idea is, poetically speaking, that of old-style playwrights, who dictatorially translate the idea into rational sequences of causes and effects. But it is also, politically speaking, one that the agents of autocracy try to implement, cynically trying to manipulate individuals and situations to engender fear, which, for them, is the only way of maintaining obedience, itself the only principle of life in common that they are able to conceive.

The chimerical figures whose descent into the abyss one may imagine thus stand opposed to the manipulators of words and men for whom the novelist must *invent* a plot, which can only be a plot of manipulation. Such is the constraint weighing on the novels that Conrad explicitly set in revolutionary circles, namely *Under Western Eyes* and *The Secret Agent*. Two stories about double agents, two novels about the unimaginable, *stricto sensu*. The inability of the honest professor of languages to invent the story of the traitor Razumov typifies a more global logic of incomprehension, in which one may recognize the caricatural version, the inverted version of the plots of the chimera. Here again, the point from which everything sets out is a form. But the plot's fillip arises through a poor interpretation of the message delivered by this form. The terrorist revolutionaries for whom the chimera is reduced to the *idée fixe* of the violent act – necessary and sufficient to be done with autocracy – imagine that the reserved air of the peaceful student, Razumov, expresses the depth of thought of a man who secretly shares their convictions. If Razumov betrays them, this stems, conversely, from an inability to imagine the motivations driving these men who think they can change society, 'as if anything could be changed'.[9] But this twofold incomprehension makes of Razumov the most unlikely of double agents. Indeed, he does totally the opposite of what his function involves: he cannot stop being irritated by those revolutionaries who tell him upon a first glance that they see in him a man in whom they can place their trust; he writes his police reports in a public garden and ends up admitting his betrayal just as an ideal culprit is found who would remove all suspicion from him. Conrad cannot imagine Razumov, and cannot understand the revolutionaries who trust him, any more than his narrator can. The only character with whom he can sympathize, the only

98

'sympathetic' character, is the 'female companion', the nameless woman moved only by the need to devote herself absolutely – to this people first encountered in the figure of a small girl in rags begging at sundown, to the young worker tortured by the police and who died in her arms, to the professor whose thoughts she copies down, and to the traitor Razumov, whom she will rescue when rendered an invalid in his last years – and who fears only one thing: not giving herself to the cause but seeing the illusions that give her a reason to live destroyed by the mean behaviour of a silver-tongued revolutionary.

These silver tongues flaunt exactly such eloquence throughout the pages of *The Secret Agent*, the unimaginable story of an anarchist attack invented by a writer who clearly states that he has never met any anarchists and is consequently unable to imagine the reasons for their actions. But if he cannot imagine their reasons for acting, he cannot really make them act; and, as a matter of fact, the big talkers who hold forth on social exploitation and emancipation in Verloc's back parlour – the apostle Michaelis, the comrade Ossipon and the terrorist Yundt – are utterly incapable of carrying out any anarchist bomb attack whatsoever. From its conception to its execution, the path of the attack passes along a peculiar division of labour. Its conception is the work of a diplomat from a foreign power that is unnamed but easy to identify as being the fatherland of manipulative cynicism, the autocratic Russian empire. This diplomat sets up the 'anarchist' attack in order to oblige liberal England to desist from its tolerant attitude toward the exiled revolutionaries. But, to strike terror in people's minds, he wants to devise an unprecedented, unimaginable plot; an attack aimed not at the expected targets – state or financial power – but at a target absurd enough to yield the idea of an enemy capable of anything. The target is therefore science, embodied in this instance by the Greenwich meridian. The plan's execution is clearly not entrusted to the doctrinaires of anarchy but instead to the double agent Verloc, whose sole motivation is not to lose the embassy subsidies he receives. In procuring the explosive, Verloc will call on a professor whose only objective is radical destruction and who cannot imagine any other means for it than the devising of increasingly perfected machines. And the explosive itself will be put in the hands of a simple-minded fellow, Verloc's young brother-in-law, who is the only 'sympathetic' being here, and the only one who the fiery back-parlour speeches could impact, but also the least capable of understanding the sensitivity of the infernal machine he is transporting. Stevie will accidentally trip over with the box. His body will be torn to shreds, the attack will be unsuccessful, and the affair will be resolved at this strictly domestic level: Verloc's wife will kill her husband to avenge her brother and will kill herself after entrusting their money to the big-talking Ossipon. Ossipon will gift it to the 'professor', to the man driven by a singular scorn for humankind and a singular desire finally to be done with it by employing sophisticated explosives. The book closes with a vision of this enemy of humankind, hidden among the London crowd:

> He had no future. He disdained it. He was a force. His thoughts caressed the images of ruin and destruction. He walked frail, insignificant, shabby, miserable – and terrible in the simplicity of his idea calling madness and despair to the regeneration of the world. Nobody looked at him. He passed on unsuspected and deadly, like a pest in the street full of men.[10]

This last judgement on the professor, apostle of destruction, is also the novelist's last judgement on the puppets he had to invent. But it would be vain to accuse him of caricaturing, out of reactionary prejudice, the anarchist militants that he himself admits to never having met. For expressed here is not only the hatred of the well-integrated immigrant in the land of liberal monarchy for the apostles and practitioners of radical destruction. It is the novelist's hatred for the characters that he had to invent in the old style, short of being able to continue to follow chimerical adventurers on faraway seas and rivers. Anarchist gossipers, autocracy's manipulative bureaucrats, 'scientists' making explosives, or the prophets of destruction – all conspire to undertake the same work of death: not only the death of liberal civilization but also that of the crazy chimera that flees liberal wisdom and gives the new fiction its subject matter. But they do more still: they oblige the novelist to become an accomplice of this destruction. They oblige him to invent stories about outrageous acts of manipulation and to give fleshless bodies to abstractions drawn from dead texts. Thus they also make of him a double agent who works on the job of inventing – of manipulating – that kills off the chimeras of the Jims, the Axel Heysts, the Tom Lingards and even the Kurtzs. *The Secret Agent*'s final paragraph contains a violence that cannot be explained in terms of political prejudice or personal antipathy. Sympathy and antipathy are not subjective feelings. They are ways of being with one's characters or of not being able to be with them. The evocation of the nihilist professor passing by in a London street, miserable and as unnoticed as the plague, is exactly symmetrical, exactly opposite to the final evocation of the chimerical adventurer Jim, tearing himself from the arms of his beloved wife to realize at last, in death, his dream of chivalrous heroism. Jim's form would inspire a whole fictional universe, a universe similar to the very incoherence of life and the chimera that redeems it. That of the 'professor' goes unnoticed against the setting of the metropolis. It engenders no universe of images and sensations. It is therefore necessary to invent a character for him and to lend to this character a possible conduct and verisimilar motivations, that is to see without truth. Faced with the demands of this invention, how can we not evoke the irrevocable judgement of Joseph Conrad, the writer, on the work of one of his colleagues around the time of *Almayer's Folly*:

> But not a single episode, event thought, word; not a single pang of joy or sorrow is inevitable [...] Everything is possible – but the note of truth is not in the possibility of things but in their inevitability. Inevitability is the only certitude; it is the very essence of life – as it is of dreams.[11]

Inventing the diplomat's cynical and absurd plans, Michaelis's humanitarian speeches or Ossipon's villainous acts – is this not to renounce the single truth of the inevitable and place oneself under the false banner of the possible? One no longer knows then, in reading the caricatural story of anarchist puppets, if one is dealing with Joseph Conrad the honest British citizen, expressing his horror of revolutionary disorder, or with Joseph Conrad the adventurer-writer, avenging himself for having been returned by his very subject to the rut of the old poetics. But there is something in this resentment that goes far beyond the personal sentiments of an author. This something is the breach introduced into the old relationship between the necessary and the verisimilar. The invented verisimilar has become the contrary of the necessary, which, for its part, is not invented, since it is the common essence of life and dreams. The verisimilar has become unimaginable: the business of manipulators and no longer of artists. The line that separates imagination from invention also separates the writer from the double agent.

Paper Landscapes

How can we recognize a fiction? Sebald's *The Rings of Saturn* tells of a journey undertaken by the author within a well-specified radius of the city of Norwich in the east of England at a fairly precise date – the end of August 1992. The author, as the reader may readily verify, was teaching at the University of East Anglia in Norwich at the time. The reader may similarly verify the reality of the places that he claims to have visited – Somerleyton Hall, the once elegant seaside resort of Lowestoft, the dead town of Dunwich, abandoned military installations at Orfordness... – and the actual existence of the colleagues he mentions or of the people he says he visited along the way – the poet and translator Michael Hamburger or the self-taught artist Alec Garrard, hard at work building an exact replica of the temple of Jerusalem. The stages of the journey provide an occasion to evoke either other sorts of journeys undertaken by the narrator, or else events from the past linked to the places visited, events no less attested: the thwarted love of the émigré Chateaubriand and the young daughter of a pastor, the splendours of Somerleyton Hall in the times of the entrepreneur Morton Peto, the visit of the eccentric Algernon Swinburne to Dunwich, the residence there of the English translator of Omar Khayyam's *Rubaiyat*... He illustrates his story with numerous photographs: memories attesting to the reality of what was seen – a Chinese quail behind fencing at Somerleyton – postcards authenticating his descriptions or archive documents illustrating his historical digressions. The book's ten episodes thus seem to comprise a poetic report on a territory and on the history that it condenses. Indeed, the author had first intended them to appear in the feuilleton section of the *Frankfurter Allgemeine Zeitung*, in which selected writers embroider an elegant arabesque of narration, reflection and reverie around a place, an oeuvre or an event. That these ten days discreetly echo Jean-Jacques Rousseau's ten *Reveries of a Solitary Walker* clearly does not run counter to that purpose.

However, the ten feuilletons that Sebald first envisaged underwent a fate similar to that of the report James Agee was supposed to write on sharecroppers from Alabama for *Fortune* magazine: it developed into one of those books deemed unclassifiable, the narration of which multiplies the digressions, freezes in the fascinated accuracy of meaningless details or dissipates in a dream that rulelessly traverses times and places. But it should really be asked whether this genre of writings, called unclassifiable out of mental laziness, doesn't define a new genre of fiction, the characteristics of which are perhaps enunciable on the basis of works such as *The Rings of Saturn*. For the book creates a series of variances that make up a system and construct the topography of a fiction, to which these gaps retrospectively prove to be the putting to work.

The evanescent contours of this topography are set from the first paragraph of the first episode. Everything begins with the journey's stated starting date: 'In August 1992, when the dog days were drawing to an end, I set off to walk the county of Suffolk [...].'¹² A date is always an indicator of reality. Of what reality it remains to be seen. When Flaubert begins the story of *Sentimental Education*, 'On the 15th of September 1840, at six o'clock in the morning', this detail does not aim to have readers believe in the real existence of the journey that Frédéric Moreau undertook that morning. It is not intended to root the story of the young bachelor in lived reality but, on the contrary, to separate it from this reality, to fix, in the ordinary course of time, a point from which a specific temporal sequence becomes autonomous. The real it is a matter of marking is that of fiction. There was a time when this marking went without saying. Fiction would make itself known via the specificity of the characters and adventures it invented and especially via its temporal structure: it matched its concept whenever the succession of events in it conformed to a causal chain endowed with a necessity superior to the unfolding of ordinary life events. This super-rationality became lost when, in the nineteenth century, the novel plunged into the universe of common things and idle time. The chain of causes and effects no longer structured the time of fiction. This time had to pertain to a single bloc, as though the breath of one and the same modality of existence ran through it.

The apparently trivial dating that opens *The Rings of Saturn* indeed conforms to this modern state of fictional time. We have no particular reason to doubt that the author actually undertook this journey following a heatwave at the end of August 1992. But neither can we ignore the relation between the time that he undertakes to put in story form and the time that, 'numbed by the idleness of Sunday and the melancholy of summer days', opens *Bouvard and Pécuchet*. Nor does anything prohibit us from hearing in the ten episodes of the professor's journey along the English coastline the echo of the ten-chapter-long explorations of the two copy-clerks, travelling the Normandy countryside in search of archaeological curiosities, or the English Channel coastline in search of geological discoveries. It is true that the account of the journey, begun under the sign of heatwaves and empty time, takes an immediate distance from the great homogeneous nappe of sentences that in one and the same breath and one and the same tonality draws in the diversity of Bouvard and Pécuchet's adventures in the land of knowledge. It is not that the professor's journey is more organized than that of the two autodidacts. To the contrary, the order of time in it is blurred from the first paragraph, since, even prior to taking us on the first stage of his trip, the narrator tells us of the nervous illness suffered a year later, in which it had resulted, and describes for us the square of sky that could be seen from his hospital room. From there, the first episode takes place as a series of digressions, leading us from the evocation of two colleagues, one a Flaubert specialist, the other a Ramuz specialist, both of whom were already dead before his stay in hospital, to a search for the skull of the seventeenth-century English writer and doctor Thomas Browne, supposedly located in the hospital museum, then to Rembrandt's *The Anatomy Lesson* and to the actual scene of Doctor Tulp's lesson, which Thomas Browne may have attended while passing through Amsterdam, before ending with the treatise that this same Browne wrote on the history of incinerations and funeral urns. The narration thus continues to move further away from the journey announced. It advances us a year and then returns us to a work written over 300 years earlier, a work devoted to a search that strayed into the night of times and myths.

But this temporal disorder strictly defines another order, which is to say a way of linking journeys, time and knowledge. This other way is at once allegorized in one of the first memories evoked by the narrator: the room of Janine Dakyns, his deceased colleague who was perhaps not by chance a Flaubert specialist. On her desk, he tells us, something of a paper landscape had formed, a scenery of mountains and valleys, which itself flowed, like a glacier, onto floorboards slowly accumulating several strata of paper that then moved back up along the walls and reflected the fading light of twilight like a snowfield. This tumbledown paper invading the floor reduced the scholar to working from an easy chair, at which she wrote on her knees, in a similar way, as the narrator mentioned to her one day, to Dürer's angel of melancholy, 'motionless among the instruments of destruction'.[13] But his colleague rejected the likening: the heap's apparent disorder was the path toward a completed order. Similarly, Sebald tells us elsewhere, for the atelier of the painter Max Aurac, a character from *The Emigrants* invented as the double of a very real painter, one whose paintings are overloaded with successive impastos, which are regularly scraped off again to make way for new ones, producing debris that covers the studio floor.

These two descriptions are also indications of Sebald's method of writing and of our manner of reading. One can always invoke mourning, trauma and melancholy regarding a book placed under Saturn's patronage, and convoke Dürer's angel and Klee's Angelus Novus, whose eyes, as Benjamin has it, are wide open faced with the pile of debris called 'progress' that 'before him grows skyward'. But we must hear the lesson of the Flaubert specialist and that of the painter who sets down to work each day to apply new impastos to his canvas and then scrape them off again. It is a matter neither of remaining motionless on one's chair nor of inscribing on one's canvas or one's writing tablet the shock of the irreparable. The destruction that the artist treats of must instead be imagined, in the manner of a Flaubert reinvented in the circumstances, as a dust cloud of Saharan sand, crossing oceans and continents only to fall again in ashes on the Tuileries Garden or a village in Normandy. The landscape of shifting paper is disorder set in action by those who refuse to be buried in the sand but also by those who stand always at the extreme edge of this vanishing. We are told this in the book's first paragraph: this false departure ends a year later in a hospital room where the vast expanses 'walked the previous summer' had shrunk 'to a single, blind, insensate spot'.[14] There is a reason for this, the author tells us. The fine freedom of movement he enjoyed during this excursion around Norwich was accompanied by a feeling of overwhelming, paralysing horror 'when confronted with traces of destruction, reaching far back into the past, that were evident even in that remote place'.[15] Destruction is assuredly this writer's concern and above all, of course, the destruction of the Jews of Europe, which is like the secret silently buried under the idyllic landscapes of the Bavarian Alps where he spent his childhood, a silence the scholar wanted to flee by going to live in England and teach at a cutting-edge university recently established in a region in industrial decline. His books revolve around this destruction, around the destiny of those who left never to return, of those who were able to flee, and notably of those children whose parents, at the very last minute, had sent them in special trains bound for England, where some lost their names and even their memories.

To this history, however, *The Rings of Saturn* bears witness in a strange fashion. In the Hamburger family's exile, having left Berlin in 1933, the most dramatic moment concerns a pair of budgerigars confiscated by English customs officers upon arrival at Dover. And the extermination is evoked only by a famous photograph in which corpses can be seen lying on the ground in the shade of the pines trees at Bergen-Belsen, that has been well isolated on a double-page spread as though it did not illustrate but rather generated the text. At this point, the text tells us of the eccentricities of a former British Army major who retired to a Suffolk property after having served in the unit that liberated Bergen-Belsen:

in the 1950s this major had dismissed all the house and garden staff, remaining in the company of a sole housekeeper, to whom he promised his entire fortune on the express condition that she shared meals with him in a state of absolute silence. The major's story comes after a long passage devoted to the fishing of herring and the symbolic meaning of fish as an emblem of nature's indestructible productiveness, and is presented as the recollection of an article about the death of the eccentric major, of whom the traveller is reminded upon seeing a brackish lake similar to that at the edge of the major's property. With the parenthesis closed, the walk continues with a climb up a cliff, the sight of a sounder of swine that recalls an episode of Mark's Gospel, and diverse visions or hallucinations at a cliff's edge that blur the real's points of reference and evoke the imaginary worlds of Tlön, summoned to erase the known world. The episode ends thus on a grand finale, in which a retrospective doubt is brought to bear on the major's story, though to confirm it, a photo from a press cutting is presented to the reader's eyes.

The press cutting seems in fact to have been invented, just like the major's story and various other of the narrator's encounters and readings. But what the story's confirmation by texts or images of ambiguous status indicates is precisely a shift in the meaning of fiction. There is no need to oppose that which a human brain has invented to that which has really existed. For the world whose reality we experience and experiment on daily is itself nothing other than the covering of the natural world by that which the human brain has produced. We live on the 'borderline between the natural world [...] and that other world which is generated by our brain cells'.[16] Bergen-Belsen, like Tlön, is an invention of the human brain. Fiction's journey to this place can be defined as the construction of a fabric able to link these inventions together. Some will proclaim it indecent to place under one and the same notion of invention the creations of an imaginative writer and the Nazi executioners' work of death. Further, as we know, the polemic continues around whether one might have the right to represent the extreme of destruction, whether stories may be made up about it, or even simple pictures of it produced. Now, from the outset, Sebald's method sweeps these quarrels aside. The question is not to know whether one has the right to represent it or not. At any rate, the work of destruction caused a suffering that exceeds our capacities of representation. This much he says, in the following episode, about Dutch paintings of naval battles. He also says this about the accounts of bombardments and cities set ablaze: the history of human suffering is ordinarily woven with stereotypes that seek to compensate for the excess of what was lived over what can be said. This is why the most convincing testimony of the destruction of Berlin is the story about the bombing of the zoo and the reactions of panic-stricken animals: elephants tugging at their chains or reptiles writhing in pain as they go down the visitor staircase. Humans have no 'lived' stereotypes of animal suffering at their disposal.[17] For this reason, too, the most telling image of the destruction of Cologne is the photograph of a street transformed into 'deep-set country lane' invaded by grass.[18] Sebald thinks it apposite to set this postwar return of proliferent nature among the ruins of German cities against the return of another natural phenomenon, 'social life': the life of people quick to 'forget what they do not want to know, to overlook what is before their eyes',[19] to construct, on the buried ruins of a will to destruction, the innocent prosperity of an economic miracle.

The work of fiction must be thought from this forgetting. At issue is not simply to uphold memory. It is a matter of constructing a memory that inserts into an accurate topography the image of the countryside in the streets of Cologne and that of bodies lined up in the calm shadow of the Bergen-Belsen pines. This topography of memory, which is equally a topography of fiction, Sebald defines as the encounter between two tectonic plates. This is the encounter that the writer's trek organizes. The nature through which he travels is not a refuge for solitary daydreamers far from human spitefulness. It is the place that bears witness to the human work of construction/destruction but equally also to the power that works continuously to destroy, in turn, the work that destroys it. The countryside visit is a journey along the fault line between the history of nature and the history of what the 'brain's nervous cells' have added to it: constructions that have destroyed or transformed nature for the purposes of human dwelling, industry or pleasure, but also those specially devised for destroying other humans. Each of them has not ceased themselves to be subject to the power of destruction specific to the bit of nature that they destroyed. And this struggle is the one whose history the fictional/memorial voyage follows. For memory consists not in memories but in traces materially inscribed on a territory. At every place it is possible to retrace the struggle between the productive/destructive work of nature and the productive/destructive work of the nervous cells of the human brain. In travelling up and down the countryside that extends between Norwich and the North Sea, formerly known, on the other side, as the 'German Ocean', and in walking along the Suffolk coastline for several kilometres, one can find several centuries of history written or buried in the landscape, and draw up a topography of the encounters and the struggles between natural history and human history. The traveller thus wanders among remnants of pumps and windmills, once so many industrious activities scattered across the countryside, but also so many stains of light throughout it, which were abandoned in the interwar period. He stops to visit Somerleyton Hall, an old feudal seigniory, which, in the nineteenth century, Morton Peto, the ephemeral king of the railways, had rebuilt as a dreamlike oriental palace with stained glasswork lit up by Argand lamps in which nature and art were confounded but whose main enchantment today stems from its clutter of useless things accumulated generation upon generation, there as if waiting to be sold at auction, while outside the trees planted by the industrialist continue on with their work of reconquest. He stops at Lowestoft, a once flourishing port, which in the times of Morton Peto's marvellous undertakings was a model seaside resort thanks to its bowling greens, botanical gardens, library, tea house and concert halls, as much as its seawater and fresh-water baths. He then heads to Dunwich, which, before being gradually submerged by waves, was a major port town with 'more than fifty churches, monasteries and convents, and hospitals in it during the Middle Ages; there were shipyards and fortifications and a fisheries and a merchant fleet of eighty vessels; and there were dozens of windmills'.[20] He comes next to Felixstowe, a destination prized by the Kaiser's family at the beginning of the twentieth century and certain to become a seaside resort of choice for the German elite had the First World War not dried up the recruitment of tourists before it ended the reign of the Hohenzollern. The journey ends, not without a passing evocation of the devastating storm of 1987, in the city of Norwich, an eighteenth-century centre for silk weaving whose fabrics appeared as nature's work itself for those who, from St Petersburg to Seville, came to behold samples of it.

Along its entire distance, this journey to the land of constructions engulfed by countryside or sea is doubled by an archaeology of bellicose undertakings. This latter begins in the garden of Somerleyton where a hypothetical gardener mentions to the traveller the seventy airfields established after 1940 on the territory of East Anglia alone. It continues on to Henstead, relating the problematic story of the major who allegedly liberated Bergen-Belsen, and then to Southwold, the bay of which, in 1672, was the scene of a confirmed naval battle against the Dutch fleet. It reaches its height with a clandestine visit to the military installations at Orfordness that took over from the defunct industries in the postwar years, before these installations, too, were abandoned, becoming a fantastical landscape of buildings in the form of temples or pagodas, the function of which became indecipherable and which emit 'the notion of a mysterious isle of the dead', the cemetery of a civilization 'after its extinction in some future catastrophe'.²¹ Thus illustrated are the walker's reflections in the heath: 'like our bodies and like our longing, the machines we have devised have a heart that is slowly reduced to embers'.²²

From each point of the coast, from each encounter or reading, real or imaginary, the circle of this 'reduction to embers' indeed seems to grow larger. A book from the disused Sailor's Reading Room in Southwold illustrates the butchery of the First World War; a newspaper read, the afternoon of that same day at the hotel, recalls the atrocities committed during the Second by the Croatian Ustashe. A television programme, which the narrator tells us he fell asleep while watching, enables an allusion to the encounter, deep in the Congo, between Joseph Conrad and Roger Casement, a man who denounced the crimes of Belgian colonization before embracing the Irish cause and then perishing, hung for the crime of high treason. This detour authorizes a new one, via another territory of violence and exile – the Poland of the young Conrad. The bridge over the Blyth, built in 1875, initiates an immense detour via the railway that crossed it at the time but that first seems to have been designed for a modernity-loving Chinese emperor: the occasion to evoke a long history of violence that covers the Taiping revolt, the opium wars, the destruction of the Summer Palace by French-English troops, and the crimes of the regent Empress.

The story of the Empress's cruelties nevertheless contains a singular moment of reverie: the sight of the sovereign calmly seated at nightfall amid the palace halls devoted to the cultivation of silkworms and 'listening devotedly to the obliterating noise, at once low, even, deeply soothing, coming from the countless silkworms gnawing on the new mulberry foliage'.[23] No doubt this obliterating murmuring evokes for the Empress only the idea of a people at work, utterly subordinated to its task. But for the narrator and for his readers it marks the point from which the chronicle of destructions may be reversed. The aim of the journey through the English countryside is not to remind us of the interminable history of human destruction. It is to weave, on this subject but also counter to it, the thread of another link between human inventions. An 'unclassifiable' book is, first, a book that returns fiction to its core. This core is not the making of plots but the weaving of the very link that enables them to be made: the link between what happens at such and such a time in this or that place and what happens in the same place at another time, in another place at the same time or at another place at another time. This return of fiction to its core is especially befitting of its object here – the history of destruction. This history is indeed the history of a certain relation between space and time: humans have not ceased building, higher and higher, edifices destined for destruction and burial and, by the same logic, weapons for the purpose of destroying and burying other humans. This history of constructions destined for destruction is what is called progress: the power that time exerts over space, the power of the force that continuously eliminates these moments, even if it means transforming this operation in movement into an end to be attained. This model of progress is also the model of classical fiction, always pulled toward the attainment of an end. Happy or painful, the end nonetheless imposes the order that is to be followed and all the eliminations required for its smooth progress. The model driving it is that of construction bound for destruction. This is indeed what the major principle of fiction posited by Aristotle encapsulates, the principle of the peripeteia that inverts the expected effects of the causal chain. If there is such a thing as modern fiction, it can be most succinctly defined by the abolition of the peripeteia. In it, time stops hastening to its end; it stops the Saturn-like devouring of its children. The 'random occurrence', formulated by Auerbach as the principle of Virginia Woolf's fiction, is precisely that: the moment that no longer builds or destroys anything, that does not reach toward any end but dilates endlessly, and includes, virtually, every other time and place. It is a time of coexistence, overcome by the liberalness of space.

This inversion is what the journey of *The Rings of Saturn* fictionalizes, in a fiction that is its own meta-fiction. Journeying is not a simple occasion to go from place to place. It is primarily a way of constructing fiction as anti-destruction, of constructing it as radical horizontality. In any given place, it is possible to contradict the process of construction/destruction to which such a place bears witness. This is possible by weaving the link that ties it horizontally to another place and another time but also by tying the documentary testimony about what this place presents to a multitude of forms of writing that weave links between presence and absence and differently knot together the modalities of the possible, the real and the necessary. At each spot, easily locatable along the coastline of a small English county, it is possible to find the point of departure for an infinite digression that ties this place and its history to a multitude of different but comparable places and times, of serious or fantastical tales, of historical documents, of collected objects bearing witness or of myths lost forever in the night of time. Digression is obligatory, it is even the rule – little matter what furnishes the occasion for it. A small brochure found on the railway on the Blyth provides the point of departure for the long Chinese episode. The books in the Sailor's Reading Room lead, if we are to believe the journeyer, as far as the attack on Sarajevo. But even the absence of a link sometimes forges the link. Accordingly, the narrator, after evoking past naval battles between England and Holland, tells us that on that very evening at Southwold's *Gun Hill* he just could not believe that a year ago to the day he had been standing on the Dutch coast looking toward England. Thus begins a long series of digressions that systematically diverts the Dutch sojourn from its declared goal – a close study of *The Anatomy Lesson of Dr. Tulp* – and extends it through diverse episodes that trace around the ill-seen painting a series of spider webs that lead us to former times or far away continents: a restless evening in a quarter inhabited by Asian immigrants; an evocation of the story of the Mauritshuis, built during the governorship of Johann Maurits over Dutch Brazil, at the inauguration of which eleven of the native Indians were allegedly brought over to perform a dance, thus reminding The Hague's bourgeoisie of the immensity of its empire; a walk toward the beach of Scheveningen on the erased traces of the enchanting landscape described by Diderot; the sight on the beach of a Kurhaus turned into a caravanserai; notes taken at the hotel about the shrine of Saint Sebald seen previously in Nuremberg; an evocation, through a reading of Lévi-Strauss, of São Paulo streets in ruin and overrun with vegetation; a group of Africans in white robes at the airport; a gentleman looking at a picture in the newspaper of a volcanic eruption appearing just like an atomic mushroom cloud; and the story of a return flight where a landscape viewed from above appears just as it always does during air travel – that is, as a territory on which humans have disappeared into the settings that they have created.

Fiction thus unfolds not as a linking of times but as a relation between places. But, further, each place is several things at once and fiction is built as a relation between several forms of reality. The Dutch journey that links several of the book's episodes at a distance is thus a multitude of journeys at once. Holland is the country on the other side of the sea; it is the land of painters and the blessed soil of the Enlightenment but also the centre of the great commercial and colonizing empire that enabled the pictural splendours and progress of the Enlightenment; it is yet the place of passage between Germany and England, a passage cited here as a touristic itinerary but elsewhere alluded to as the route of Jews fleeing Nazism to asylum on British soil. Lastly, it is the other bank of that mythological river of the dead, which the journey does not cease to cross from each point of the coastline. This journey endlessly extends the circle of destruction, but its loops also continually weave a multiplicity of circles of circles, a space of coexistence that leads back towards a sensible world that is common to the living and the dead, to illustrious existences and to anonymous lives, all those whose lives were devoured by the work of construction, all those that the work of destruction never ceased to make disappear.

For the problem is not to link everything with everything. It is to weave a territory of coexistence similar to the Pisanello fresco that Sebald evokes in *Vertigo*, and which he praises for its capacity to 'create the effect of the real, in which every feature, the principals and the extras alike, the birds in the sky, the green forest and every single leaf of it, are all granted an equal and undiminished right to exist'.[24] A right is nothing in itself. What counts is the work performed to make it effective. And this work is precisely that of new fiction. This is the work that another geographical detour from the coastal walk, the Ireland detour, simultaneously accomplishes and allegorizes. Indeed, an unverifiable dream in a hotel introduces a long digression narrating the narrator's hypothetical stay in a dilapidated Irish residence whose occupants history has forgotten and who themselves have, in turn, forgotten history. We may choose whether or not to believe in the reality of this sojourn. But the real of fiction is elsewhere: it is in those cones of paper with which their owner, he tells us, would dress the heads of faded flowers and then tie a thread around the stems. After which

> she would cut off all the stalks, and bring the bagged heads indoors and hang them up on a much-knotted line that criss-crossed what was once the library. There were so many of these white-bagged flowerstalks hanging under the library ceiling that they resembled clouds of paper, and when Mrs Ashbury stood on the library steps to hang up or take down the rustling seed-bags she half-vanished among them like a saint ascending to heaven.[25]

If this picture creates fiction, this is neither because it is invented nor because of the picturesque quality of the description. It is because it is linked with other stories about murmurings and collections that traverse the episodes: the fabric ends gathered by the Ashbury ladies to make useless multicolour, patchwork bedspreads; the silkworms' murmuring as they consume the leaves on the Empress's mulberry trees; the collection of fabric samples conserved in the small museum of a Norwich manufacturer; the unending labour involved in constructing a model of the temple of Jerusalem; and the Flaubert specialist's mountains of papers that, flowing down from the tables to form glaciers and climbing back up from the floor, themselves refer to the mountain of papers that the collectors Bouvard and Pécuchet gathered with the sole aim of feeding their daily work of copying, which is also their inventor's work of writing.

One must therefore not be misled about the episode's meaning: if the collector of seeds is there, it is not as a curiosity arresting the amused look of a journeyer. Besides, this journey may well have never taken place. But the narrator, who perhaps never set foot in the Ashbury house, knows as we do that virtually everywhere on territories marked by the violence of history and the destruction of progress there are collectors and bricoleurs of this kind who apply themselves to a rather precise work: to create life from that which is dead, the new from the used, art from industrial materials, history from insignificant events and almost erased traces. In sum, to contradict and redeem the work of destruction. The episode therefore holds both as an example of these multiple undertakings and as an apologue of the specific work of the writer: the latter's task is not to hang small picturesque cones on a string, but to stretch tight the thread that unites the cones of the botanist landowner with the academic's mountains of paper, the self-taught artist's temple, the writings of the polygraph doctor Thomas Browne in all domains of knowledge, or even the funeral urns celebrated by one and the same Browne, cheerfully mixing archaeology and mythology, grand hypotheses on the history of civilizations and a fascination for objects contained in urns, a passion for the regularity of geometrical figures and an attention to the anomalies of nature. Over the entire surface on which exploitation and domination have stretched the web of their destruction, one can spin another web by interweaving a multiplicity of horizontal and egalitarian links. The story of the silkworms, covered in the last episode, reminds us of this. On the one hand, this story can encapsulate the entire history of capitalism's subjugating of nature and harbouring all manner of disciplinary dreams. On the other hand, however, this is already turned upside down in a famous text written by the very author of *Capital*: the silkworm, says Marx, is a particular type of worker because its production does not adhere to the law of so-called productive work, that is to say, of work that disappears in surplus value. This is why its work may symbolize the poet's labour.[26] This is also why its story can symbolize here the counter-work of fiction, scouring spaces not to collect rare objects but to invent another image of time: a time of coexistence, equality and the inter-expressiveness of moments in opposition to that of succession and destruction.

This other image of time is already sketched in the book's first, apparently trivial sentence, where the author tells us he had set off as the dog days of summer were drawing to an end to escape the emptiness growing in him upon completing 'a long stint of work'. This jaunt is announced as that of an academic on holiday, which is also to say as one at variance with a certain practice of science. Indicating this variance is an almost insignificant detail, the reference to the dog days, days that are placed in a subsequent passage under the sign of the Dog Star, a catalyst for diseases of body and soul. Here again we need not ask whether the author really believes that the stars have an influence over human destinies. It suffices here that this reference engenders another use of time from that of classical fiction with its events governed by the end-to-be-realized, but also from that of science which, by continually absorbing the facts of production and destruction into the causes of which they are the effects, contributes to the work of production/destruction in its own way. Astrology suggests the image of a link that subtracts from the fictional and scientific empire of the productive/destructive linking of causes and effects. A link that, by the same token, is subtracted from all hierarchy. The point is not that everything is equivalent and that all orders are good. Even travelling in the countryside, the author of the new fiction is still like the weaver or the writer 'pursued, into their dreams, by their feeling of having got hold of the wrong thread'.[27] But precisely the right thread is to be found in another cartography of time, not one of a cause-and-effect governed chain of succession. Now, calendar time provides the simplest image. For this time is not the pure succession of things that occur idiotically, one after the other. Each date of a calendar is separated from the order of succession and refers to something else other than itself: to events arising at diverse places on a same day of the year, in a more or less distant past; to the history of a patron saint or a mythological divinity; to tasks or moods of the season; to diverse pieces of information or stories specially composed at the end to instruct, entertain or delight all those who otherwise endure the routine wherein each day is like every other.

One of Sebald's great inspirations is to be found in the almanac stories of Johann Peter Hebel. Sebald aims to wrench these everyday stories from a Heideggerian thinking of rural rootedness and make of them the model of an egalitarian crossing of experiences, languages and kinds of knowledge. Hebel's predilection for parataxis and coordinating conjunctions is not, Sebald tells us,

> indicative of a homespun naiveté; rather it is precisely the way he deploys these particles which gives rise to some of his most sophisticated effects. Opposed to any hierarchy or subordination, they suggest to the reader in the most unobtrusive way that, in the world created and administered by this narrator, everything has an equal right to coexist alongside everything else.[28]

Accordingly it is in the mode of parataxis that Hebel's stories come to be inserted into the professor's journey along the Suffolk coastline. The sight of a hearse in the streets of the declining town of Lowestoft jogs the walker's memory, reminding him of 'that working lad from Tuttlingen, who, two hundred years ago, joined the cortège of a seemingly well-known merchant in Amsterdam and then listened with reverence and emotion to the graveside oration although he knew not a word of Dutch'.[29] This unidentified worker – who first admires the wealth of tulips and wallflowers featuring on the window sills of a beautiful residence, then the abundance of crates filled with colonial products amassed in the port, before noting that the owner of these riches does not escape any more than he does from the fate of mortals – is straight out of a Hebel almanac story, 'Kannitverstan', which Sebald explicitly evokes in *A Place in the Country*. The worker in it is an apprentice from Germany who arrives in Amsterdam and asks, in German, after the owner of this superbly flower-decorated palace, to which his interlocutor replies, in Dutch, that he does not understand the question. The apprentice takes the reply for the owner's name, a certain Mr Kannitverstan, whose crates of goods piled up in the port he enviously admires, before he meets a funeral procession and, asking the identity of the deceased, laments, on receiving the same reply, the sad fate of this Mr Kannitverstan.

We ought not to be misled about the moral of the story. It is not the equality of all faced with our mortal condition that Sebald asks us to admire in the short story by Hebel, but rather the equality that his writing simultaneously produces and promises. It is the work of language that 'constantly checks itself, holding itself up in small loops and digressions and molding itself to that which it describes, along the way recuperating as many earthly goods as it possibly can' and whose sentence endings open, independently of any programme of social equality, onto a horizon of fraternity.[30] To redeem the work of destruction and contradict the work of domination, it is necessary to introduce into the very composition of fiction those detours, digressions and about-turns and those sentence endings located at the edge of the void that the German chronicler would introduce into language. It is necessary to introduce them to bring down the confines from within which a text gets addressed to one type of readership distinct from others and to open as broadly as possible the fraternal space in which experiences communicate across differences in genres of writing: articles from scientific encyclopaedias or regional press articles, pamphlets by local scholars, erudite works attesting to the different ages of science, almanac stories, pedagogical or other booklets. All this material – the same that cluttered the desks of Bouvard and Pécuchet as well as their author's – must be moved through via the threads of a new fiction. This new fiction identifies the moving from place to place and from moment to moment with the work of a mobile sort of thinking that itself mixes genres and transforms the story of walking into a reverie, a hallucination, a fantastical dream, a parable, a memory of reading, a mythological visit to the land of the dead, an invention of imaginary journeys or of fictive encyclopaedias, in order to 'salvage all it can' of shared experience and broaden the fraternal spaces of coexistence of places and times, of experiences and sentences.

This network of community, which fiction must trace, can be thought through from a single remark made by Sebald on discovering that the Jewish émigré landlord who took him in in Manchester twenty years earlier had skied, prior to fleeing Nazi Germany, on the same Bavarian slopes that the young Sebald had skied down some years later. 'He left traces in the snow on the same hills', he comments, going on to say that from these common traces history lessons may be drawn that no textbook includes.[31] Fiction is, in short, the work that makes (up a) hi/story by linking some erased traces in the snow with other erased traces in the snow. It entails a particular mobilization of knowledge. This knowledge must dispense with its ordinarily assigned, petty function of explanation, and thus of suppression, not in order to yield to some sort of brute stupefaction before the irruption of the real, but to enter into an order of metamorphoses where it variously divides and modulates and becomes, at one and the same time, matter for fiction and a fictional form.

This is perhaps the ultimate moral of the story of 'Kannitverstan'. Not understanding is not a deficit. It is an interruption in the dominant mode of the process of production of meaning that incessantly rationalizes the work of destruction. One may certainly understand the link between the flowers on the balcony and the crates piled high in the port, between these crates and the violence of colonial exploitation, and between the lofty words of religion and the order that sanctions this violence. But knowledge of such, by which the work of destruction is denounced, does not redeem it. It continues to follow its logic by dissolving in its turn the vividness of flowers and that of beautiful sermons into the production and distribution of surplus value. It is necessary to know how to ignore this knowledge in order to create an egalitarian link between the window flowers, the beauty of words and the wonder of artisans that conserves each one alongside the others in their equal right to existence, but that also enriches them by transforming them into translations, echoes and reflections of one another, and in principle also of other translations, echoes and reflections to infinity. This is another use of knowledge, one that produces not only a new sort of fiction but another sort of common sense which links without subordinating or destroying.

The Edge of the
Nothing and the All

The Random Moment

At the end of *Mimesis*, Erich Auerbach, a scholar scarcely inclined to making grand statements, praises a book in which he sees not only the supreme crowning of western literature but the promise of a 'common life of mankind on earth'. Of books dealing in the torments and hopes of humanity in transformation, there is assuredly no shortage. But the one that Auerbach picks out would seem to be far from a great epic of the human condition. In question here is Virginia Woolf's *To the Lighthouse*, whose story is limited to an evening and a morning, both made up of small, insignificant events that transpire in a family circle in an island holiday home. And the passage on which Auerbach comments to justify his statement relates the most trivial of domestic events: the mistress of the house, Mrs Ramsay, is inside knitting a pair of socks for the lighthouse-keeper's son and trying them out for size on the legs of her own young son.

How might this summery evening among a petty bourgeois family announce the future of humanity? Two chapters earlier the same Auerbach defined the heart of modern novelistic realism, which, as he put it, can represent humans only as inserted in a rapidly changing global political, economic and social reality. This global reality has apparently dissolved within the space of two chapters. But what seems to have also disappeared along with it is that chain of actions forming a whole that comprised the very core of fiction. The accomplishment of western realism hailed by Auerbach strangely resembles the decadence of the realism Lukács had deplored ten years earlier and that he identified with an overturning of the hierarchy between narration and description. The core of authentic realism had, for him, to show things from the point of view of active characters, in the dynamic of their action. The ends they pursued and the confrontations in which they engaged made it possible to grasp the global social movement embedding their action. When, in *Lost Illusions*, Balzac described an evening at the theatre to us, he did so from the viewpoint of his hero, Lucien de Rubempré, who employs his quill both to promote the show in which his mistress, Coralie, is playing and to cement his own position as a modish journalist. This narrative mode would enable the reader to perceive, through the rise and fall of an ambitious youth, the long hand of capitalism extending at once to theatre and to journalism. But this conjoint dynamic of narrative action and revealing a social process was already lost by the time of Zola. The author of *Nana* described to us in minute detail all the aspects of the theatre at which his heroine performed: the performance, the audience, the set changes, the work of the dressers and so on. But we were thus provided merely with a succession of tableaus, of 'still lives' presented from the passive point of view of a spectator and no longer from that of the characters in action. This losing of novelistic action in passive description subsequently intensified in the works of Joyce and Dos Passos, to the extreme point of a fragmentation of experience in which the inner life of the characters is itself transformed into 'something static and reified'.[1]

At first glance, Auerbach takes the same path in going from *Old Man Goriot* to *To the Lighthouse*: a path that turns away simultaneously from the constructed arrangement of fictional plots and from the common life of humans. Yet, Auerbach's interpretation of this development inverts the perspective: Virginia Woolf's micro-story does not divert us from what is at stake in the human community. On the contrary, it opens onto the future of this community, toward the moment when humanity will live 'a common life on earth'.[2] But if it does so, it is not *despite* but *because* it ruins this arrangement of actions hitherto regarded as the very principle of fiction: 'What takes place here in Virginia Woolf's novel is precisely what was attempted every-where in works of this kind (although not everywhere with the same insight and mastery) – that is, to put the emphasis on the random occurrence, to exploit it not in the service of a planned continuity of action but in itself.'[3]

This statement is extraordinary: the supreme achievement of western realist fiction is the destruction of that 'concerted chain of actions' that appears to be the minimal condition of all fiction. This destruction lies in the privilege afforded to the *random occurrence*, which he also calls the *random moment*. How are we to conceive of this achievement, which takes the form of radical destruction? And how does the reign of the random moment presage a new common life on earth? Auerbach only answers the above with some banal considerations on the content of these random moments, which concern 'the elementary things which our lives have in common'.[4] But he has said enough about it previously to allow us to perceive that the 'common' at stake in the random moment does not concern time's content but its form. If there is a politics of fiction, it does not arise from the way it represents the structure of society and its conflicts. It does not arise from the sympathy it might arouse for the oppressed or from the enthusiasm it may generate in the struggle against oppression. It arises from the same thing that renders it fiction, that is to say, a way of identifying events and linking them with one another. The treatment of time is the core of the politics of fiction.

After all, this point has been known since Antiquity, Aristotle having given it exemplary expression in the ninth chapter of the *Poetics*, in which he explains why poetry is *more philosophical* than history. This is so, he says, because poetry – by which he understands not the music of verses but the construction of a fictional plot – says how things *can* happen, how they happen as a consequence of their own possibility, where history only tells us how they arrive one after the other, in their empirical succession. Thus tragic action shows us the chain of necessary or verisimilar events by which humans pass from ignorance to knowledge and from fortune to misfortune. Not merely any man at all, it is true, but men who are of 'great reputation and prosperity'.[5] To go from fortune to misfortune, one must belong to the world of those whose actions depend on the chances of Fortune. To undergo this tragic adversity, which is due not to vice but to an error, one must be able to commit errors and therefore to put forward grand designs, the means for realizing which may draw one into error. The poetic rationality of necessary or verisimilar linkages applies to those men who are referred to as being *active* because they live in the time of ends: those ends that the action puts forward but also that end in itself constituted by the privileged form of inaction called leisure. This time is here clearly opposed to the time of so-called passive or mechanical men, not because these latter do nothing, but because all their activity is enclosed in the circle of means that aim at the immediate ends of survival, a circle in which inaction itself is only ever the rest that is necessary between two expenditures of energy.

Constructed fiction is more rational than described, empirical reality. And this superiority is that of one form of time over another. These two Aristotelian theses formed the dominant rationality of fiction for centuries. They established it on a hierarchy that did not need to be argued for because it belonged to the sort of self-evidences around which a world is structured: the hierarchy of forms of life that distinguish 'active' men from 'passive' men by their way of inhabiting time, by the sensible framework of their activity and their inactivity. The following question can then be raised: was this hierarchy of forms of time that upheld the rationality of fiction destroyed in the modern age? Did Marxism not turn the game upside down? With Marxism, precisely, the dark world of the production and reproduction of life became the world of causal rationality. Thus defined on the basis of its core – the production of material life – history opposes its rationality to the arbitrary arrangements of fiction and opens, to those who grasp its laws, onto the future of a humanity without hierarchy. But inverting an opposition entails retaining its terms and the structure of their relationship. And even if, in *Capital*, the game that science and history play is a complicated one, the Marxist science of history reprises at least one principle of fiction for its own account, transmitting it to a posterity that carefully erased its aporia: that of the hierarchy of times. This science is undoubtedly no longer the vain knowledge acquired, albeit too late, by a tragic hero who falls from fortune into misfortune. On the contrary, its possession is supposed to give one a view of global connections and the means required to adjust means to ends. But it does so only by opposing, once more, the time of active men, who grasp the linkage of causes and inscribe their undertakings within it, to the time of passive men, whose material occupation obliges them to remain in the cave, in which things only appear one after another, in a contiguity that nothing ordains, except perhaps the mirage of ideology.

As a form of account, the Marxist science of history remains Aristotelian. And it so happens that whenever it takes literary fiction into consideration, it weds its order of reasons to the old fictional hierarchy. Lukács does just this when he opposes two forms of time: the time of the authentic realist novel, that of 'complete personalities' who, by pursuing their ends at their own risk, reveal to us the structure of social reality and of historical evolution; and successive time, the reified time of 'still lives' of the naturalist novel or the Joycean fragmentation of experience. The Marxist theoretician of literature thus takes up on his own account the hierarchy that opposes active men to passive men. And perhaps Auerbach senses this complicity even as he links the 'serious realism of modern times' to the representation of humans 'embedded in a total reality, political, social, and economic, which is concrete and constantly evolving':[6] this constantly evolving reality only works to reproduce time and again the separation between those who live in the time of causes and those who live in the time of effects. Hence, perhaps, the oddness of the examples with which Auerbach illustrates his remarks; indeed, all of them are counter-examples, that is examples of places and times in which this 'constant evolution' seems to be suspended: the musty dining room in the Maison Vauquer in *Old Man Goriot*; the ennui of the diners at the Hôtel de la

Mole in *The Red and the Black*; that of the lunches in *Madame Bovary*'s damp dining room. This apparent contradiction has its logic: 'serious realism' is also, and even primarily, one that breaks with the ancient separation dooming the representation of small people to low genres such as comedy or satire. This realism turns them into subjects susceptible of having the most profound and complex sentiments. There is the second major principle that must find its accomplishment in modern literature. And symbolizing this are indeed Julien Sorel, the carpenter's son out to attack the social hierarchy, and Emma Bovary, the daughter of a peasant out to vanquish ideal passions, both of them 'serious' until death sanctions their desire to live a life other than that reserved for people of their social condition. Now, living another life means, first, inhabiting another time. And *ennui* is the entry into that other time. It is the experience of empty time, a time not normally known to those whose ordinary existence divides between the work that sustains and the rest that restores. This is why it is not simply a frustration; it is also a conquest, a transgression of the division separating humans into two according to their way of inhabiting time.

Just as one awaited their meeting, the two criteria of the realist accomplishment separate. The man of the people asserts the capacity to be the subject of an intense and profound drama only by being detached from the network of relations that would include him in a global reality in becoming. The hierarchy of times and forms of life is not broken on the side of global social reality, but, on the contrary, on the side of its suspension, by the entry of random individuals within this empty time that dilates into a world of unknown sensations and passions. Unknown to the imprudent men and women who scorch their wings and their lives in contact with this world, but foreign, too, to fiction, which discovers here an unprecedented mode of the being of time: a temporal fabric whose rhythms are no longer defined by projected goals, the actions that seek to accomplish them and the obstacles that set them back, but by bodies that move to the rhythm of hours, hands that wipe the mist from windows to watch the rain fall, heads that prop themselves up, arms that fall down again, known or unknown faces that come into view behind windows, furtive or resonant footsteps, a musical air, minutes that glide over each other and melt into a nameless emotion. Such is the time of Emma Bovary, of that ordinary day from which Auerbach excerpted the famous lunch.[7] For the heroine, who does not know what awaits her and does not know that this non-knowledge is itself a new pleasure, this is a time of despair. But, in any case, this is a new time for fiction, released from the expectations it knew all too well and introduced, on the contrary, to the infinite multiplicity of minute sensations and nameless emotions making up lives subtracted from the hierarchy of temporalities.

This path is likely that which causes fictional democracy to veer from the grand history in which the science of history naturally saw it located, toward the universe of sensible micro-events. The democratic revolution of fiction is not the grand and sudden emergence of the masses on the stage of History. It is nevertheless faithful to the modern definition of revolution: this latter being the process by which those who were nothing become all. But becoming all, in the order of fiction, is not about becoming the main character of the story. It is about becoming the very fabric within which – through the stitches of which – events hold together. The grand revolution that Auerbach indicates without defining it takes place when the fabric by which events hold together is the very same one by which events happen to those to whom nothing ought to happen, those who are supposed to live in the infraworld of reproductive time, in the cave where things simply happen one after another. The random moment is not simply one of the essential activities in which all humans engage. And the promise of humanity contained in Virginia Woolf's random moments does not consist in there being everywhere in the world at the same instant women who knit and are busy with their children. It is not time's content that is overturned but its very form. The time of the representational tradition was two-dimensional, with each dimension defining a form of exclusion. First, it excluded on its horizontal axis, by making each moment disappear into the succeeding one. Second, it excluded on its vertical axis, by separating those who lived in the world of action from those who lived in the infraworld of repetition. By contrast, the random moment is the element of a doubly inclusive time: a time of coexistence in which moments interpenetrate and persist by spreading out in larger and larger circles; a shared time that no longer knows any hierarchy between those who live in it. Illustrative here is another of Virginia Woolf's novels, *Mrs Dalloway*, the story of a single day in which the walks around London taken by a worldly woman, her daughter and her former lover experiment with a new space-time, in which the same sensible events spread out step by step, affecting all bodies similarly and notably those that the old order kept at a distance or made invisible.[8]

But the random moment is not only the indifferent atom of this time of coexistence. It is also the turning point that stands on the precise boundary between the nothing and the all, the moment of encounter between those who live in the time of shared sensible events and those who live in the outside-of-time, in which nothing is shared or able to happen. Thus the circles of the shared random moment woven on London streets in the morning around the elegant Clarissa Dalloway, out to buy flowers for her party, come to a standstill in two limit figures. There is, emerging from an underground entrance as though from the depths of the earth, a trembling form, similar to a rusty pump, whose voice of no age and no sex murmurs an unintelligible song without beginning or end. And there is that young man, dashed in his poetic ambitions and traumatized by the war, whose delirium transforms the fabric of random sensible events into the revelation of a new religion that he must proclaim to the world. This young man, Septimus, will throw himself out of a window to escape from the doctors who want to place him in an asylum. We know that his act prefigures the novelist's own, since she will also escape from madness and doctors by committing suicide. The proper task of 'realist' literature is, then, to transcribe the power of these turning points between the event and the non-event, speech and silence, sense and nonsense, under its two figures: the stupidity of the lack of sense and the madness of the excess of sense. It is to construct with words a common world that includes separation itself, that links the directed time of Clarissa Dalloway's day and of the passers-by she meets with the frozen time of the 'old rusty pump' chanting near the underground entrance or with the disoriented time of Septimus. But this inclusion of the excluded is neither the abolition of differences in a universality transcending them nor the recognition of their peaceful coexistence. It is the violent inclusion in a form of sensible community of the same thing that makes it explode, the inclusion in a language of that which escapes this language. Such is what may be meant by that 'foreign language within language' claimed by Proust and commented on at length by Deleuze: the transgression of the ordered division of voices and idioms, that transgression which attains its ultimate point with the inclusion in language of the impossibility itself of speaking.

The random moment, in reality, is not random. Most certainly it can be produced at any instant for any insignificant occasion. But it is also the decisive moment, the moment of turning that stands on the exact boundary between the nothing and the all. 'It was nothing. Just sound.' – says Faulkner, speaking, in *The Sound and the Fury*, of the groan of the idiot Benjy. But he immediately transforms this nothing into an all: 'It might have been all time and injustice and sorrow become vocal for an instant by a conjunction of planets.'[9] To stand on that boundary on which lives that will tumble into nothingness are elevated to a totality of time and of injustice – this is perhaps the politics of literature at its most profound. One would like to see such a politics send combatants off into battle, to accompany the victorious movement of the historical process. But perhaps these stories that seem to stand so feebly in their variance from the grand tumults of History-on-the-march perform a more radical displacement that challenges the temporality within which that battle and its victory are conceived. It fell to Walter Benjamin to give this displacement its political meaning by affirming the necessity to separate the 'tradition of the oppressed' from the time of the conquerors with which Marxist theory had united it and to tie the dialectic no longer to the advances of time but to its arrests, its overlaps, returns and conflagrations. But already before him certain literary works had performed these ruptures, which stymie the victories of History by holding onto that edge of time, that boundary of the nothing and the all on which the division between active humans and passive humans is blurred. For this, their authors undertook to condense and dilate times, to fracture them, to recompose and intertwine them, thus reducing the time of conquerors to being only one among others and reducing its necessity to the particularity of one scenario among others, one simply poorer than others.

Thus, reality does not stand counter to fiction, rather fiction stands counter to fiction. And this battle of fictions cannot be reduced to an opposition between a learned literature destined for the elites and the ordinary chronicle of facts. Yet it does take place wherever the issue is to establish the setting of what makes for common reality. During the summer of 1936, the young journalist James Agee was assigned by his magazine to investigate how Alabama sharecroppers were coping with the crisis. The formula required to answer the magazine's request is familiar: to interweave some small meaningless facts, which prove simply that we are dealing with ordinary lived existence, and signs that make sense, that is to say consensus, by showing the hardship endured by the poor and the way that these sorts of people adapt to it through a combination of resignation and resourcefulness. Things thus fall into place and reality remains the same as itself. But James Agee did something else. During the day, he would unpack the contents of all the sharecroppers' drawers and show in each pin or in each piece of fabric the all of a way of inhabiting the world. During the night he would listen to the breathing of the sleepers; in this light breathing he hears not only the break that has come after the day's heavy weariness but the injustice of all the lives that might have been lived; he ties this breathing to the noises of the surrounding night, to the multiplicity of lives that breathe everywhere at the same time, to the softness and the violence of the starry sky and of cosmic respiration. He constructs a 'conjunction of planets' that wrests these lives from the verisimilitudes of social reality and from the necessities of globalized time to give voice to 'all time and injustice and sorrow'. To the time of the conquerors, to this horizontal and continuous time today described as 'globalization', the new fiction opposes a broken time, traversed at each instant by these points that raise no matter which nothingness to the height of the all.

Two Stories of Poor People

At the centre of the fictional topography of *Light in August* there is a man seated behind his window. He monitors the street, says Faulkner, who has not unintentionally given this watchman the name of Hightower. But what is to be monitored in this ordinarily deserted street? What novelty can he really see through this window buried under vegetation and offering no view other than a half-dozen low-growing maples and a faded sign? What counts about his being behind this window is, first, his motionless position. The position, it might be said, of someone waiting. However, so much time has elapsed since he last waited for a student to come to the art lessons advertised on the sign; so much time since he last sat himself down there, alone, after being chased out of the church, whose pastor he once was, by a long series of scandals: his exalted sermons, which seemed to confound the Saviour's glory with the cavalcade of an ancestor who had waged war there during the civil war; the misconduct of a spouse, found dead in a seedy hotel room in Memphis; the presence of a black servant alone in the widower's house; and various other incongruities. From behind his office window, it is not visitors he is watching out for, not the spectacle of passers-by that he is observing, but the sound in the distance: the sound of his church during service – no doubt, for the prayers, the sermons, the songs from which he has been excluded, but primarily for the sound of hatred and death that resonates there.

The organ strains burst forth like ecstatic crucifixions, their sound waves 'pleading, asking, for not love, not life, forbidding it to others, demanding in sonorous tones death as though death were the boon',[10] echoing the rumours of hate that cross through the crowd of honest people, gathered there less to honour the Crucified than to ask for more crucifixions: of sinners, of people belonging to that other race and of those who mix with it, and lastly of themselves and the curse that carries them away in a spiral of hatred. From behind the windows, there is nothing to be deciphered and nothing is able to surprise. There is only a tonality to be felt. From afar, the watchman hears the muffled murmur of the continued curse. He sees in spirit the crucifixions to which it never stops giving form.

But if he listened from afar for the sound of hatred only, there would be no story. For there to be a story, the immobile man must have visitors pass by his door, bringing the drama to a place that, in normal times, only rumour can reach. The visitors in question are not simply any old visitors, but those through whom the scandal, and therefore the story, happens. But the scandal is split into two. First, there is the ordinary weakness of the flesh, to which the country girl, Lena Grove, succumbs, seduced in her lost hamlet in the darkest depths of Alabama by one of those light-hearted journeymen who travel from place to place renting out their arms and knocking up girls. To find the man she cannot imagine a liar, she sets out on the road, on foot, heavy with the child about to be born. This scandal, easily resolvable with a good marriage, is introduced into Hightower's office by a good man, the Good Samaritan Byron Bunch, who imagines himself a Saint Joseph. But the more radical scandal that emerges comes not from the weakness but from the hatred of the flesh: hatred of the sinful temptress, hatred of those who, through this fault, are born of impure blood. As the cart that welcomed Lena and the child in her womb arrives in Jefferson, a glow of a fire lights up the sky: a house is ablaze. It is Miss Burden's, that lover of Blacks and daughter of a carpetbagger, murdered by her young lover, the octoroon Joe Christmas, whose blackness was not to be seen on his face but the secret of whose curse the orphanage's dietician divulged to him after he inadvertently caught her in the act of making out with a colleague. From his window, Hightower is unable to see the fire's glow. But he will see the drama's actors come in through his door one after the other: first of all, shown in by Byron, Joe's grandfather, the imprecator who took from his daughter her new-born Joe and placed him on the orphanage doorstep, born as this child was of a sinner's impious fornication with a man of the Devil, namely a quadroon who managed to pass off his brown skin as that of a Mexican; and lastly, entering by force, Christmas comes in, the accursed child who inherited his father's black blood, his mother's weakness for the flesh and his grandfather's hatred of the guilty flesh of woman. In Hightower's residence this white-camou-flaged negro will not only be killed but emasculated by the executant of decent people's fury, National Guard member Grimm, himself frustrated that the world war came too early for him. This is how the story or, rather, the two crossed stories enter into the immobile watch-man's house.

One might say that this is not a good way of telling things. The solitary Hightower has nothing to do with the ordinary misfortune of Lena Grove or with the monstrous destiny of Joe Christmas. And this latter might have been caught and killed absolutely anywhere else. But we must take things the other way around and ask why the novelist wanted these two fates, which no reason bid to cross each other, to cross where they had no need to, in the house of the motionless watchman. Indeed, the novelist multiplies the tours de force so that the fallen pastor can be placed centre story, even as he appears in it only at distant intervals. Thus does his accredited visitor, the very discreet Byron Bunch, inform him in all improbability of the crime and the investigation, leaving the reader to wonder how Bunch himself had learned about them. Everything transpires as if the narration ought, at the price of verisimilitude, to be arranged around this motionless point; that is, the zero point of the story, that of the man to whom nothing can happen any longer and who simply hears the background noise of old-time stories, the sound of the ancient and ever young curse. What ties both stories together is not their common character, Lena's fleeing lover who becomes Christmas's accomplice; it is the existence of this motionless point at which their destinies cross. Both destinies have a common point: both happen to the kind of individual to whom, in the fictions of yesteryear, nothing ever happened. But the ways in which they break with this normal destiny of immobility and invisibility are diametrically opposed. Lena's story is a story of modern times. She belongs to that new age in which the most minuscule of beings, things and events have acquired a fictional dignity, not because novelists have a particular tenderness for the little people but because their minuscule stories permit fiction to play on the quasi-imperceptible boundary between the nothing and the something. Lena's sin of sleeping with a travelling worker and her misfortune in falling pregnant result from no defiance or attraction to evil, but simply from a careless mistake and rotten luck. What eventuates is not a curse, but merely the decision to set out on the road and ensure her child has a father. And Lena's story can be entirely summed up by this overland trip, which is modest but nevertheless rather incredible to her. She who, though initially destined never to move and aware she was bound to remain wherever she arrived for the rest of her days, at the end marvels at having made the journey from Alabama to Tennessee in only a few months.

Fictional democracy takes this first form, the minuscule story or Lena's simple furrowing in a straight line, similar to the cart, whose apparently motionless movement the first pages of the book describe. And there is, by way of Christmas, the other story of democratic times. Here, it is not the novel that approaches the almost nothing of ordinary existences; it is these existences that show themselves worthy of the stories of sound and fury that, in old times, only struck princely families. But if they can do this, it is because added to the ancient malediction of accursed races and enemy families is a modern form of curse which very especially affects the poor: indeed it strikes those who have veered from the well-worn path of popular existences and sought to live the life reserved for those who found themselves on the other side – the daughters of peasants who, like Emma Bovary, sought to experience an ideal and passion-filled life, or sons of the people who, like Septimus in *Mrs Dalloway*, wanted to become poets and lettered. As for Christmas, he wanted very little; he wanted only, at five years of age, to taste the dietician's toothpaste. However, his bad luck meant that he was in hiding in her room right when she yielded to her colleague's advances. The error is most certainly fairly minor, but the line it crosses is more redoubtable than the separation of classes and enjoyments. Without wanting to, the little Joe violated the only principle capable, as the old servant Dilsey in *The Sound and the Fury* would have it, of ensuring the salvation of black children: do not get mixed up in the affairs of the Whites; keep your distance from the matters of hatred and fury that are the lot of those

despoilers who took the land of the Indians and subju-
gated the Blacks. Now, this principle is not one that
the small child cannot fail to transgress for the simple
reason that he does not know himself to be black, which
is something he will learn when, for his punishment, he
is chased from the paradise of white orphans. But the
error, of course, had preceded him, with the sin of his
mother, the curse of his grandfather, the long history of
despoliation and hatred in the South and, at the end of
the chain, the curse that had always befallen men for
having wanted to lay their hands on the knowledge of
good and evil reserved for divinity.

Such are the two intersecting stories of poor people:
one that reduces the melodramas involving seduced
and abandoned common girls to almost nothing; and
the other that, conversely, summons the entire chain
of curses afflicting the human race. This cross-over
clearly entails a particular poetics. The novelist – who
has read Flaubert and Conrad and knows that there
is now an interest in recounting the most obscure life
– doubts, despite it all, that the straight line drawn by
little people like Lena Grove can provide enough for a
novel rather than a simple novella. He doubts that the
novel can abandon the ancestral formula of fiction as
a passage from fortune to misfortune. And he knows
that the time of the moderns, a time that is readily
said to be condemned to the freneticism of speed, is,
on the contrary, too slow, too attentive to the weight
of each second, to ensure the brutality of that passage.
However, even the latter is no longer what it was in
Aristotle: a paradoxical chain of causes and effects born
of a simple error. It has returned to being what it was
before him: the inevitable curse weighing on a family
or a race. This line is another straight one but one that,
from the outset, runs headlong toward the expected
catastrophe.

For there to be fiction, the lowly story of innocent Lena Grove must cross the ignoble story of Joe Christmas – who, like Oedipus, is guilty even before being born – at the risk of the former, in turn, opposing her quiet minimalism to the immemorial stories of hatred and murder. Everything transpires as if Whites and Blacks had switched stories, and as if Lena had adopted the wisdom of the old Dilsey, the wisdom of not mixing. But their stories must also meet in the residence of a man who is motionless at his window. Forty years earlier, a writer of whom William Faulkner indeed seems to have been aware, Maurice Maeterlinck, encapsulated the revolution of fiction in a simple opposition. The old stories of filiation, love and hate – jealous husbands killing their wives, fathers immolating their sons, sons murdering their fathers, assassinated kings and raped virgins – seemed to him to reflect the unrefined conception of the world of another age. New drama, as he saw it, was conversely embodied in the silent attitude of an old man 'sitting in his armchair, simply waiting beneath his lamp, listening, without realizing it, to all the eternal laws which rule over his home, interpreting without comprehending what there is in the silence of doors and windows and in the small voice of the light'.[11] Faulkner made a decision to reject that opposition between old and new fiction, too unschooled in the modern violence of filiation and race whose inheritor he knew himself to be. He nevertheless retained the figure of the man who listens seated at his window. But he turned him into one who hears not the silent murmur of destinies but the sound of hatreds and curses that form the basis of every story. And he combined the new fiction with the old, by making the motionless man's armchair the meeting point between Lena Grove's modest voyage and Joe Christmas's journey unto death.

The Mute's Speech

Faulkner's *The Sound and the Fury* is known by two essential traits. The first is the complexity of its temporal structure, which comprises disordered comings and goings that occur on three days in 1928 and one day in 1910. In keeping with this temporal disorder is the story's being split between four narrative voices: one objective account and three subjective narrations, one of which is confided to the student Quentin Compson, who is living his last day before his planned suicide, and two others to his brothers, the cold calculating Jason and the idiotic Benjy. Benjy's narration, we know, opens the novel and lends it its tonality. The role given to the idiot is the second of the book's notable traits. The question that thus arises is: how are we to understand the apparently paradoxical relation between the complex and sophisticated temporal structure of the novel and the weight taken in it by the brute speech of an idiot, of a man supposed to be living in the immediacy of a present bereft of background. To answer this we must dismiss the interpretation according to which the privilege given to the idiot is a literalization of the famous line from Shakespeare's *Macbeth* from which the book gets its title: 'Life is a story told by an idiot, full of sound and fury, signifying nothing.' On this interpretation, Faulkner simply took the sentence at face value by putting the narration in the mouth of a born idiot who is unable to understand what he sees or coordinate what he feels. And it is this lived reality of a being affected only by sensible shocks devoid of reflection that the narration allegedly espouses.

This 'face value' is nevertheless trickier than it would appear. Indeed, one thing catches the reader from the first sentence. The present in which Benjy lives is straightaway separated from him. The idiot speaks in the past tense and he speaks not about what he sees but about what he could see in what was his meadow in times past and what is today a golf course: 'through the fence, between the curling flower spaces, I could see them hitting'.[12] From the first sentence his position is that of someone who recounts, someone who parts with his present by recounting it. And in the space of a single page, he will recount three different scenes situated at different moments. Admittedly, it could be said that this time of separation is, from another point of view, a mark of inseparation. The preterite would then function as a language pertaining to a confusion of tenses, a language of an unending past. And the commonly done thing is to reduce this past to the primitive scene and the *es war* of the unconscious. But the preterite used in the first person by Benjy comes from another source. Faulkner himself put us on the trail by saying that his novel is the work of a reader who discovered only by writing what he owed to authors he'd read long ago without thinking further of it: Dostoyevsky, Conrad and Flaubert. He uses a preterite that incorporates into the English language, as Conrad had already done, a tense that does not exist in it. This preterite incorporates the Flaubertian imperfect, a tense which the French novelist himself had diverted from its grammatical function and turned into a mood apt to blur the distinctions between moods, by homogenizing the course of observed events with that of states of consciousness.

This import at the same time contains an essential deviation. In Flaubert, homogenization had one condition. It could only take place in the third person, which it transformed into the impersonal voice of narration: the stupid voice that expresses what there is without reason, like a swirl of dust in the wind; the ontological stupidity of a universe that does not pursue any end. Flaubert contrasted this ontological stupidity with ordinary stupidity: the self-importance of wily operators, who always find reasons for that which has none and deem themselves masters in being able to make these reasons serve their own ends; that is, like Homais, enlighten the ignorant, or, like Rodolphe, seduce idiots. Even if the voice of the 'reasonable' man Jason recalls Homais's wisdom, Faulkner's dramaturgy cannot be one of an opposition between two stupidities. For fatality, with him, is not, as it is in Flaubert, pure chance, the pure 'stupidity' of a whirling of atoms; it is a causal linking that always refers to an older damnation. Benjy's idiocy is part of the same heritage as his father's alcoholism, his mother's hysteria, his uncle's parasitism, his sister's and his niece's sexual addiction, the incestuous fantasies of his eldest brother and the sly reasoning of his other brother. On the other hand, the idiot's voice does indeed come to be inhabited, in the first person, by the Flaubertian stupidity of the impersonal voice. How else are we to understand the singularities of his monologue? How might we even understand the simple fact that the idiot faithfully retranscribes the words being exchanged around him, words he ought not to understand, including those that tell of his being deaf and dumb? The deaf and dumb person who speaks is the voice of impersonal writing that takes into its homogeneous tissue the moans and groans of the idiot at the same time as the words that turn around him. His monologue, as one can easily note, has many traits in common with that of his brother, Quentin, the Harvard student, whose sentences are sometimes ampler and more ornate but sometimes also even more disjointed than his. Quentin describes to us what he 'could see' in a parataxic way as well. His monologues also comprise an inextricable confusion between present and past, perception and memory, the speaker's voice and that of others. Benjy's speech does not stand out in this sense from the monologue of 'normal' people. Besides, this is why his narration must regularly be supplied with practical indications that remind us that the person speaking is, in the literal sense of the term, an idiot: a physically disabled individual who needs someone to hold his spoon when eating soup, an intellectually disabled person who expresses his sensations only through groans or cries of rage. But this recalling can only be done at the price of recreating distance between the subject of the narration and the animal of which it speaks.

Far from the novel borrowing the voice of the mute idiot to state the absurdity of life, it conversely grants another sort of mutism to the one who does not talk. It grants him the 'mutism' formerly denounced by Plato, the voice of impersonal writing that removes from speech any directed course and denies all hierarchy among speaking beings. This enables the novel to lend articulated speech to the unintelligible chant of the 'old rusty pump' on which, in Virginia Woolf, the happy circuit of the shared sensible moment founders. It is not a matter of saying through an idiot that the world is idiotic. It is a matter of transforming, through writing, the idiot's sound into human speech. The novel's work as a whole might be encapsulated by two sentences found in its last part, in which the narration is objective, so that, naturally, Benjy does not speak, because objectively a deaf and dumb idiot does not speak. He groans, at most. And this is indeed what the narrator tells us here by relating to us the groan that Benjy makes heard. 'It was nothing', he tells us, 'just sound'. But the following sentence transforms this nothing into the virtuality of a whole: 'It might have been all time and injustice and sorrow become vocal for an instant by a conjunction of planets.'[13] In this simple sentence are simultaneously condensed and put into question the two major oppositions that have served to hierarchize humans on the basis of their ways of being and speaking, the oppositions formulated in parallel in Aristotle's *Poetics* and in his *Politics*. There is the opposition between two times: that of the chronicle, which only says how things occur one after the other, and that of fiction, which says how they *can* occur. And there is the equally famous opposition that founds the political community by separating two uses of the vocal organ: the animal voice that signals the pleasure or pain being experienced, and the human *logos* that enables the just and the unjust to be made manifest and put up for discussion. This totality of normally silent injustice, which is voiced for an instant, evokes those dramaturgies of politics in which the beings held to lack speech gain a voice, not only to tell of their suffering but to affirm their capacity to speak – and to speak about justice. An exemplary scene of this sort is the secession of the Roman plebeians on the Aventine Hill, as rewritten by Ballanche during the modern revolutionary era. To make the justice of their claims heard, the plebeians first had to make it heard that they spoke. They had to make it heard by the Patricians – for whom this was a physical impossibility: what came out of plebeian mouths contained no speech but only, as one among the Patricians said, 'a fugitive sound, a sort of bellowing, a sign of need and not a manifestation of intelligence'.[14] Faulkner's two sentences about the idiot's groan provide us with a sort of original scene of literature, one symmetrical to the original scene of politics as figured by the story of the plebeian secession. Symmetrical and dissymmetrical simultaneously. For, clearly, to prove that he speaks, the idiot will not take up speech 'himself'. It is the writer alone who sets himself the task of uncovering 'all time and injustice and sorrow, become vocal for an instant by a conjunction of planets'.

This is the specific form of dissensus that literature enacts with its words. Politics enacts dissensus in the form of speech collectively taken by those who intend to provide the proof that they speak. Literature, for its part, gives singular speech to those who cannot evince it, to those who are absolutely unable to speak. The speech that the novel lends to Benjy is not the brute speech of the idiot – speech about his pain; it is a voiceless speech, speech about a more profound and more distant justice. By identifying the voice of the mute with that of silent writing, Faulkner's novel enacts its own justice. It constructs the sensible world in which this complaint is understood as discourse: a sensible world that includes its contradiction. What the paradox of the idiot's writing entails is indeed not a simple compassion for the victims. It is the existence of this common time and of the common world that Auerbach saw heralded in Woolf's random moment. And Auerbach undoubtedly speaks about it in an overly simple way. For the common is in fact always a tense relation of the common and the non-common, of the shared and the unshareable. Claiming to be the same for all, the time of the victors thus works ever so effectively to drive to its margins and into its asylums all those ill-adapted to its rhythm. As for the fiction of the idiot, it advances another articulation of the common and the non-common. On the one hand, it lends the idiot the enriched, deeply multiplied time that stands opposed to the monochord time of the clever. On the other, it maintains, like a wound at the heart of the common world, the irreducibility of the separation between idiots and normal people.

In this tension between the common and the non-common, the singularity of the idiot's monologue is articulated with that of the plurality of stories. Echoing the idiot's monologue from afar, which is to say in the

North of educated people, is the student Quentin's monologue, which contains the same confusion of times and voices. Contrasting with this are two straight-line narrations that cannot comprehend his speech. There is the objective narration that only hears him as moaning and groaning, and there is Jason's monologue, that of the third brother and reasonable man who works to provide for his family basically by engaging in dubious short-term speculations on the money market with money that is not his own. Jason is the man who does not confuse times, the man of economic rationality and history's linear progress, in which idiots and the ill-adapted more broadly – all those who are unable to adapt to its rational march – are shoved out the exit door. The individual voice of Jason is the other Flaubertian stupidity, the voice of Homais-type rationalizers. At the end of *Madame Bovary*, the reader will recall, Homais's great concern is to have the blind man sent to the asylum, his hideous face and soliciting presence on the public way being an insult to the progress of civilization. The time of Jason is also extended to the moment at which each person will occupy the place handed down to him: at which Jason will finally be a master in his own home and the idiot will occupy the place that quite naturally awaits him – the asylum. The complexity of the novel's narrative structure, with its splitting of voices and times, serves to delay indefinitely the moment when he will be able to carry out this wish. It serves to retain the idiot in a common time and world and, along with him, all those that the time of the economy and power, the time of victors, to reprise Benjamin's words, pushes continually to the margins, to spaces outside place and times outside time.

The splintered time of writing delays the linear time of History, the time belonging to the Rodolphes, the Homaises and the Jasons, the time that increases the resources of rentiers, hands out honours to publicists and sends the disabled to the asylum. This is where the modest and timid politics of new fiction is played out. Fiction does not put forward solutions to cure the disabled. But it does arrest the hands of those who send them to the asylum. It keeps the disabled present by indefinitely delaying, through the time of writing, the time of reasons which sends them to the place where they will be locked up. The 'random moment' is not only the moment of condensation unique to the infinite resonances that, during the times of Chekhov or Maupassant, the novella isolated, like a window half-open onto a world of ignored lives and emotions. It is also this power of splintering, the power of multiplication that causes dominant time – that of the victors – to explode at the very point of its most assured 'victory': at the edge of the nothing, to which it relegates those who are outside speech and outside time.

The Measureless Moment

'This is the story: a little boy went.'[15] Thus begins the first of João Guimarães Rosa's *First Tales*: with a boy who takes a plane to go and see the construction site on which, in the semi-wilderness, the great city was being built. The tale is called 'The Thin Edges of Happiness'. In the twenty-first story, titled 'Treetops', we again discover this ageless and nameless boy taking the same journey. The story comes quite naturally to an end with the plane's landing as it returns. 'We're here at last', says the uncle accompanying him. 'Oh no, not yet', replies the boy, as if desiring to remain an instant longer in the time of the story, to delay what comes at the journey's end: 'And life was coming.'[16]

Everything thus seems to occur in the narrow interval that separates the story from the point from which it comes and to which it returns: life. And yet the story befalling the boy affords us barely any spectacular events. What ordinarily comprises the subject matter of stories is here thrust to the margins, transformed into a simple cause of, or pretext for, the journey: in one case, the future of the great city's building; in the second, the mother's illness, on account of which the child is sent away. With each occasion the journey itself is condensed into a moment's bedazzlement: in the first story, there is the 'edge of happiness' – the joyous shore – afforded by the sight of a turkey prancing about in the courtyard, a joy soon quashed since the animal was there only to meet a more trivial satisfaction, that of the guests invited for a birthday dinner. And, in the second, there are the treetops, the happiness provided by a toucan who, for about ten minutes at exactly six o'clock each morning, comes to splash the dawning day with colour and thus to announce not that the mother is cured but that she had *never* been ill, that she had been 'borne safe and sound'.[17]

We must not be misled about the meaning of the story: the point is not to contrast the childlike taste of the marvellous with the prosaicness of ordinary life. For that matter, the turkey in the courtyard and the toucan in the tree are effectively more real than the urban projects or telegrams relating the mother's news from afar. But nor is the point to contrast small lived facts with grand events. It is a matter of defining the gap through which stories arise, through which the story is written as differing from, but also as belonging to, life and composed of its materials.

The 'First Tales', or stories, could mean exactly that. Indeed, these stories are not the first ones that João Guimarães Rosa wrote. And he would not hesitate to publish his 'Third Tales' despite his second tales never having existed. No more than he would hesitate to call one of his stories 'The Third Bank of the River', even though a three-banked river seems inconceivable. The third bank, in fact, is rather its middle, but it is a singular middle that has become an immobile bank, the middle of a pond-river that heads out to no sea. The first stories are to be understood in this way. They are the edges of stories, quasi-stories that draw the edges of any story, the moments when life is separated from itself by being recounted, by being transformed into a 'true life': a life that has precisely no edges and that thus contravenes the Aristotelian principle of fiction – to have a beginning, a middle and an end and to be guided from the first to last sentence by an organized succession of causes and effects. João Guimarães Rosa does not aim to contrast traditional fiction with some supposedly modern autotelic logic. More than anyone else, he holds fiction to be a function of life – and especially, he says, of that life of the *sertão*, in which, once livestock and crop requirements are met, nothing else is to be done in some fazenda separated from its neighbour by several leagues than to make up stories.[18] But, rightly, the life of the *sertão* – without history, populated with stories – must have been lived to know that life is not made fiction in the Aristotelian manner. And perhaps it is necessary to have some 'critical tales',[19] some quasi-stories or experimental fables of the nothing and the almost nothing, of someone and no one, of the event and the non-event, to show how life is imperceptibly and radically separated from itself, how it becomes 'true life' by crossing the limit that separates *what happens* from *what there is*. The gap, precisely, is not what one habitually believes to be that which usually gives rise to the story. For this reason the first form – the simplest one – of the critical story involves a story that is expected but does not eventuate. An 'expected' story is one deduced from a situation and from the characters to be found in it. In 'Famigerado' ('Notorious'), for example, the narrator is asked for his 'opinion' by a horse rider who, with a forbidding face and arms ready for a fray, comes accompanied by three henchmen.[20] Upon hearing this horse rider state his name, a name known for leagues around to belong to a pitiless killer, there are grounds to fear the worst concerning the sort of opinion he is after. Yet the reason for the consultation is purely linguistic: this violent man wants to know whether he should feel insulted by a young, greenhorn government fellow who has qualified him as 'Notorious'. And he will leave in good spirits after the narrator assures him, before his three witnesses, that the word simply means *celebrated*, *famous*, *well known* and carries no pejorative connotation in and of itself. The subject of the quarrel, the subject of old-style stories in which one killed to avenge oneself for an insulting word, is thus defused. Now it is resolved through the opinion of a linguist.

In 'The Dagobé Brothers', by contrast, a bloody outcome seems unavoidable. The eldest of a gang of four evil brothers is to be buried. He was killed by an honest man in an act of self-defence, but that changes nothing as to the violence to be expected from the three others. In life, one anticipates what will happen next in a story insofar as one knows *how far* individuals can go in accordance with what they are. So, when the honest murderer, to prove his good faith, suggests that he might be the fourth pallbearer, those present can only deplore the madness of this young man, who has just further provoked the *how far*, as if 'what had already happened' was not enough.[21] The story is thus built upon the common formula of suspense, the question being to know at what moment that which one knows must happen will actually happen, a moment that narrative art consists in delaying to enable the tension to reach its peak. In this story, this moment arises when the body is in the grave and the three brothers are at last free to employ their arms for other things. Yet, at this point the event is brushed aside. The eldest of the survivors simply says what *happened to be the case*: their brother was a devil. And therewith the three of them take their leave of this site of tales and move to the big city. The story of the 'Dagobé Brothers' will have been an exemplary non-story: a liquidating of old-style stories – not simply of matters of endless vengeance but of stories in which there are situations and characters that hold within themselves a future that can be known.

'True' stories are therefore those in which the game is no longer about linking what is anticipated and what happens. The very subject of the tale here enters into contradiction with the necessity, which is anyway its own, to extend itself between a beginning and an end. It is carried out in an outside-time, the time of the unbegun, which, by definition, cannot be stopped. These tales around the almost nothing, which form the core of *First Tales*, may evidently be read as containing so many philosophical or religious allegories. Negative theology and learned ignorance, Franciscan starkness and the mystical union of contraries, all constantly suggest their interpretative lenses to the reader's mind. Commentators have not forgone recourse to them. And on occasion João Guimarães Rosa holds out his hand to the exegetes by granting them the plainly clear Christian analogy of a young man dressed in white, appearing in the aftermath of a major earthquake and performing a few discreet miracles and blessings before re-ascending to another fatherland.[22] But if this highly cultured man bore so well in mind all the doctrines that his stories were prone to illustrate, he clearly also bore in mind traditions of tales, fables and legends. And what his stories talk to us about is fiction itself, fiction and the suspension that it entails: not simply the suspension of disbelief – the simplest one, all-too-simple – but the suspension of that which had sustained belief itself; that is, the usual order of time, the customary way of occupying a space, of identifying oneself as an individual, of inscribing oneself in relations of filiation and of relating to forms of use and to objects of possession. The reference to the *sertão* as a place of natural fabulation ought not to mislead us: fiction is not the treasure that simple beings pass down from age to age along with family heirlooms and traditions of the land. It is the capacity to begin, time and again, the leap into the unbegun, to cross anew the edge and enter into spaces where an entire sense of the real is lost along with its identities and its points of reference.

This space is, for example, the fazenda, which serves to frame the novella exemplarily titled 'No man, No Woman'. The justification of this title is twofold. First, none of the story's characters has a name; but it may also be that they have never existed except in the head of the person seeking to reconstitute a story that seems to him to have occurred in a faraway house in times past, but to whose truth no witness can attest. The very identity of this 'recollecting' character is doubtful: throughout the story he is named 'the boy' in the third person, before he himself adopts the first person at the last moment – that of his return to the family house from which we never saw him leave – making him the indistinct narrator of his memories. And the characters whose – possible – story he recounts themselves have no proper names: around the boy there are – or allegedly were – the man, the young girl – apparently the daughter of the man – the young man (where from?) who is in love with her and the old bedridden woman around whom the story is built. She is 'Nenha', the one whose negative name says only the absence of name, identity or even precise place within the generational order. Indeed, no one knows any longer for how long this old lady, who does not recognize anything or anyone, has been there, lying in her bed like a child in a crib; no one knows whose mother, grandmother or great-grandmother she is or was. If the young girl is presented as the legendary princess in her tower, the old lady, for her part, is a princess in the castle tower who has returned to childhood, by dint of never having been woken up. She is a pure existence, extravagant, irresponsible, 'visibly enduring beyond all the purlieus of ordinary life and old age, in perpetuity'.[23] And this immobilized life prohibits the normal, happy end point of the tale: that the young girl marry the young man whom she loves and by whom she is loved. This young man's desire is the normal desire of a 'simple man' eager to 'live an ordinary life, using his own resources and following plain roads'.[24] To this desire, the young woman opposes hers, which is also her duty: to remain alongside the old woman, in whom life has been forgotten, to remain steadfast to a life not subject to change, immobile to the ultimate immobility of death.

This life, in which nothing happens, is not simply the desire of a young woman remote from the world; it is the paradoxical place of fiction, the place without history in which stories may unfold. The young woman is the guardian of fiction, the guardian of this true life whose possibility must always be preserved within ordinary living itself, but whose line of separation must also be indefinitely redrawn. Joining up at this point are the story of the boy seeking to remember and the story of impossible love whose object it is. There has to be a life in which everything mingles and in which nothing is forgotten. There has also to be a time in which the boy, who has become a 'person', enters with the other characters into one and the same indistinct life. But ordinary life obeys a law of separation and forgetting. 'No Man, No Woman', in short, sums up in a few pages the moral that *In Search of Lost Time* unfolds over seven volumes: forgetting is the sole condition of memory; the absence of love is the place at which stories of love unfold; and true life is that which exists only in the margins of life, through a rupture of the temporal relations in accordance with which individuals depend upon one another.

'No Man, No Woman' ends with the boy's emitting a cry of fury at his parents, whose lives unfold in the time of ordinary life and who mundanely want to know if he has carefully looked after his belongings and brought them back: 'You don't know anything, anything, you hear. You have forgotten everything you ever knew.'[25] However, in 'The Third Bank of the River', it is the father himself who, though a sound and calm man, heads out in a canoe he has built for the purpose to the place where one forgets forgetting. In ancient mythology, Lethe was the river of forgetting across which the souls of the dead had to travel to be able to shed the memory of their previous lives and prepare themselves to enter into a new body. But literature is not mythology. It does not have you pass from one bank to another. It holds itself in the middle, in an interval that is itself without an edge. The unthinkable third bank of the river is this middle where the passage itself no longer passes. One day, without explanation – except perhaps one given to a witness who, of course, has disappeared – the father takes the path of this paradoxical middle. The problem is not whether it is possible to survive in a canoe in the middle of the water. Ancient religions would place means for survival in the barque of the dead, and the son discreetly deposits foodstuffs on the shore to serve this same function. But the father has not left for the bank of the dead. He has gone to the middle of the river, the middle at which that which comprises the very reality of every river is cancelled out: the fact of flowing into another river that, in turn, flows into the sea. For this barque, invisible most of the time, always reappears in the same place. The middle of the river is the inexistent point where Heraclitean paradoxes are refuted by a superior paradox, the point at which the river does not flow. Such is the unthinkable event, overwhelming, that the tale relates: 'what had never been before, was'.[26] The father chose to remain 'in that stretch of the river, halfway across'. This driftless excess, this immobile crossing of the law of 'what there is', stands as an enormous question mark over those who, like the simple young man from 'No Man, No Woman', engage in 'ordinary living', as that which flows from the past toward a future. Such are here his daughter who gets married, becomes a mother and runs away with her husband far from that father of hers who does not want to see his grandson even from afar; then his wife who ends up going off to live with her daughter. It is the son, the narrator, who remains alone on the bank of ordinary living beings 'with all life's cumbrous baggage',[27] as the guardian of one who has withdrawn to the middle, to the outside-time. Accomplishing his role as a guardian, however, requires even more of him. He is obliged to become the inheritor, the successor, of one who, by going to take up his place in the middle of the river, has rejected all filiation. This is the exchange that, standing on the bank, the son suggests to the father seated in his canoe. The father seems to accept it, but the son, when the time comes, shirks from enacting it at the last instant. The story is thus doomed to end on a twofold absence. The father disappears for good, the son remains at the shore. He is 'one who never was', one who will henceforth 'remain silent', remain in the silence.[28] 'True life' does not know itself; it is destined to remain in the interval between absence and silence, between two lost inexistences and at the bank of the river that flows ever to separate them.

To draw as far as the edge of silence, the edgeless edges of that absence – that is the work of fiction. This is the work it accomplishes and simultaneously renders imperceptible by confiding it to its characters, the reasonable and methodical mad people whose extravagances calmly undo ordinary life's points of reference. In 'Nothingness and the Human Condition' this work is accomplished by the man 'no one really knew', the fairy-tale-like king hidden behind the appearance of the character least fitting to fiction's enchantments: a wealthy and honest landowner. Upon his wife's passing, Uncle Mam'Antônio withdraws 'into ambiguous spaces and moments'.[29] But he does not go as far as the interval nor shut himself up in any secret room. His project, on the contrary, is to completely clear an area of which his property is the centre, which ultimately means to make a space without property. Encapsulating this is the maxim that he adopts as his catchphrase, that he presents to his daughter's painful questions about life's vicissitudes, and that he always uses as an explanation to the workers carrying out his project: '*faz de conta*'. 'Make believe', says the translation. But at issue is not consenting to a semblance, suspending disbelief to one's own advantage. Once again, what must be suspended is the belief in 'what there is'. What the father's extravagance suggests is the creation of the de-familiarized, de-domesticated space of true life: a space extending to the peaks, a space to which a gaze can go when it faces no obstacles – in short, the space of the tale. To this end, Mam'Antônio mobilizes roadworkers and gardeners to flatten the mountains, and destroy the clumps of trees and flower beds that the reasonable, deceased spouse had once enjoyed. His daughters indeed come to find themselves excluded from this space, quickly married off to sons-in-law who will take them to live far away. But Man'Antônio will also exclude himself from it, as little by little he gives all his possessions to those who gravitate around him – servants of all skin colours, field hands and cowboys – before vanishing himself, his body becoming ashes in the final bonfire that devastates the house. Fiction thus devours its impossible place, at a distance/in the middle, consuming the extravagant characters that it brought to exist for a moment.

Not that there cannot be happy fictions nor felicitous ways of figuring its work, that is to say the nothing that separates our condition from itself. Contrary to the lover rejected by Nenha's guardian is the young man of 'Cause and Effect'. In a moment of self-evidence, this young man finds the love that he did not seek but that was nonetheless waiting for him in the dwelling of a Sleeping Beauty of whose existence he was unaware, led there by one he was following most prosaically: simply a fleeing cow, a cow that knew, for her part, exactly where she was going – to her former owners. Following the small cow who was 'surpassing her destiny' meant taking the chance to enter into 'the unbegun, the undecided, the disoriented, the necessary'.[30] This moment of encountering the unbegun is intensified in another story. In 'Substance' it becomes the very temporal texture itself – a love story that is as improbable as it is happy between the timid *fazendeiro* Sionésio and the miserable Cinderella, daughter of a leper and of a woman of easy virtue, who is employed in the court of the fazenda to do the tough work of breaking the hard cassava, with its eye-dazzling white flour, on the slab. The cassava's glaring whiteness is all that is needed for the prince to recognize the princess in the servant and for both of them to come together, advancing where they stood still, in the place and time suited to the happiness of true life – of fiction: the event of the non-fact and of non-time, 'living at the vanishing point and never stopping'.[31]

The limitless point, the immeasurable moment, of course, extends its infinity only as close as possible to the end point at which every story told must end. Not because the sad reality of life gives the lie to the illusions of fiction. But because the end itself is a means of paying tribute to the capacity of fiction through which life infinitizes itself. Every story is, then, two things at once: a leap of the infinite into the finite and a passage from the finite into the infinite. Two stories, rather different in their tonalities, encapsulate this: 'Hocus Psychocus' and 'Soroco, His Mother, His Daughter'. The first tale is about a secondary school, where, excited at being chosen to perform in the play at the school fete, some boys are busy rehearsing under the direction of a teacher. Other boys are curious to know what the play is about, so in order to keep it a secret, the chosen boys invent and spread a false story, the upshot being that the jealous boys make up a third story. Performance day arrives and an unexpected incident obliges the prompter, who is also the narrator, to assume the lead role, and so the teacher has to retreat to the prompter hole to take his place. As this happens, the troupe's loose cannon begins to act out the wrong story, the one made up by the jealous boys, to which the protagonist and his partners respond, of course, by playing out their own 'wrong story', made up to keep the teacher's story a secret. The vertigo of this battle of stories overcomes the audience and the actors on stage who, having forgotten who they were, are 'transformed' beyond all belief,[32] taking flight in love, in words, in the very equivalence of these latter – that is 'true life' – until the point at which the hero becomes gripped by anxiety: how to end this time that no longer goes by? The unending happiness of words cannot put an end to the unending happiness of words. A single solution remains: to walk while talking to the front of the stage, to the edge of the edge, and somersault into the audience. After which point the world stops; after which point, tomorrow, the usual games resume: the battle of fists to find out which story was the best.

Contrasting with the secondary school farce, seemingly, is the lament of 'Soroco, His Mother, His Daughter'. Here there is no dramatic expectation or being surprised by extravagant behaviour. The drama has already been played out. And no 'madman' has to impose his scenario of true life and arrested time. The madwomen here are 'real' madwomen, Soroco's mother and daughter; and for them, arrested time, time without beginning or end, is simply what awaits them in Barbacena, the city of the lunatic asylum, to which they will be taken by a train carriage with barred windows. The account thus seems to be merely the story of an end without beginning, the effect of a misfortune that, for these sorts of people, has always been. It seems it can be reduced to the anonymous crowd's farewell ceremony to these nameless unfortunates. But something more happens. Almost nothing. Her arm aloft, the young madwoman begins to sing: a tune with neither a right key nor precise lyrics; a song similar, then, to the rusty pump noise emitted by the ageless and sexless creature from *Mrs Dalloway*, as well as to the idiot's moan in *The Sound and the Fury*, namely, the *nothing* that the novelist forthwith transformed into a *whole*. Now, this false tune that no one can identify, this senseless concentrate of time and injustice that seems definitively to confine the young woman in her madness, will, in João Guimarães Rosa's story, produce entirely the opposite effect. It will spread from mouth to mouth as if on an opera stage. At the moment of departure, it is taken up again by the mother, with a voice that slowly grows stronger, accompanying her granddaughter in an interminable song; those present will not become clearer about the lyrics but they will be able to recognize a story of 'the great vicissitudes of this life, which can hurt you for any reason at all, anywhere, early or late'.[33] Then, after the wagon has moved off, Soroco suddenly takes it up on his own, before the crowd also joins him like a choir in unison and sees him to his empty house. 'We were going with him, as far as that song could go', says the last sentence of the story. But as it happens there is no limit to this 'as far as'. The senseless song, the song of misfortune shared across the line separating rational people from the insane and those who are still there from those who will never again be there, now extends endlessly into the interstice of the random occurrence. By blurring the division between human song and the sounds of beasts or things, it holds those who are no longer there forever in a common world. The madwoman went beyond anything that might have been expected of her, and the crowd's solidarity followed her by going beyond its expected forms, by beginning to sing the song that it was unaware of, by becoming this song itself. Fiction is that by which the *as far as* is exceeded. The choir of anonymous individuals accompanying the lone man to his empty dwelling is there to remind us: fiction's excess is not the illusion that consoles in the face of reality, but neither is it the exercise of the virtuosity of the clever. It belongs to the capacity that life has, among the humblest and most common people, to be carried beyond itself in order to take care of itself.

Literature reaffirms in its specific way the capacity to invent belonging to each person: to the madwoman who makes up her song, to the *sertanejo* who makes up his stories, and to the writer who makes up their stories. Those who say that 'the literature of writers' is pointless, since the people of the *sertão* will not read it, simply mean to say that nobody ought to recount stories, that everyone should simply believe *what there is*, simply hold fast to what is. The writer's article of faith is that the *sertanejos* would cease to tell stories if he ceased to tell their stories. This article of faith is one that no cultural sociology can investigate in order to verify. This is why the writer himself must verify it, and there is only one way to do this – by writing.

Notes

Introduction

1 Erich Auerbach, *Mimesis: The Representation of Reality in Western Literature*, trans. Willard R. Trask (Princeton: Princeton University Press 1991), p. 459.

2 On this topic, see notably Jacques Rancière, *The Politics of Literature*, trans. Julie Rose (London: Polity, 2011) and *The Lost Thread: Essays in Modern Fiction*, trans. Steven Corcoran (London: Bloomsbury, 2017).

Doors and Windows

1 Armand de Pontmartin, 'The Bourgeois Novel and the Democratic Novel', *Le Correspondant*, 25 June 1857.

2 Stendhal, *The Charterhouse of Parma*, trans. Margaret Mauldon (Oxford: Oxford University Press, 1997), p. 86.

3 Honoré de Balzac, *Le Cabinet des Antiques*, in *La Comédie humaine* (Paris: Gallimard, 'Bibliothèque de la Pléiade), vol. 4 (1976), p. 796. [Translator's note: all references to Balzac's works are to this French edition and the translations given are a select mixture of existing English translations with my occasional modifications.]

4 Balzac, *Une double famille*, ibid., vol. 2 (1976), p. 20.

5 Balzac, *Une fille d'Ève*, ibid., vol. 2, p. 263.

6 Ibid.

7 Balzac, *Le Curé de village*, ibid., vol. 9 (1978), p. 654.

8 Balzac, *La Maison du Chat-qui-pelote*, ibid., vol. 1 (1976), p. 52.

9 Balzac, *Ferragus*, ibid., vol. 5 (1977), p. 794.

10 Balzac, 'La Bourse', ibid., vol. 1, p. 413.

11 Balzac, *La Peau de chagrin*, ibid., vol. 10 (1979), p. 136.

12 Charles Baudelaire, 'Crowds', in *Paris Spleen*, trans. Martin Sorrell (London: Oneworld Classics, 2010), p. 22 [translation modified].

13 Charles Baudelaire, 'The Eyes of the Poor', in *Paris Spleen*, p. 53 [translation modified].

14 Gustave Flaubert, letter to Edma Roger des Genettes, July 1862, *Correspondance* (Paris: Gallimard, 'Bibliothèque de la Pléiade'), vol. 3 (1991), p. 236.

15 Victor Hugo, *Les Misérables*, trans. Julie Rose (London: Vintage Books, 2008), p. 939.

16 Aristotle, 'Rhetoric', in *The Complete Works of Aristotle: The Revised Oxford Translation*, ed. Jonathan Barnes (Princeton: Princeton University Press, 1984), III 11, 1412a 19–22.

17 [Translator's note: readers wishing to consult the English translation of Maupassant's *La Rempailleuse* will also find it translated under the title *Lasting Love*.]

18 Guy de Maupassant, 'The Chair-Mender', in *Guy de Maupassant's Short Stories*, trans. Bree Narran (London: The Anglo-Eastern Publishing Co., 1923), p. 34.

19 Ibid., p. 35 [translation modified].

20 Marcel Proust, *In Search of Lost Time*, vol. 2, 'In the Shadow of Young Girls in Flower', trans. C. K. Scott Moncrieff (New Haven/London: Yale 2015), p. 302.

21 Marcel Proust, *In Search of Lost Time*, vol. 1, 'The Way by Swann's', trans. Lydia Davis (London: Allen Lane, 2002), p. 162.

22 Ibid.

23 Rainer Maria Rilke, letter to Clara Rilke, 25 February 1907, in *Letters of Rainer Maris Rilke, 1892–1910*, trans. Jane Bannard Greene and M.D. Herter Norton (New York: W. W. Norton & Company, 1945), p. 263.

24 Gustave Flaubert, letter to Louise Colet, 26 May 1853, *Correspondance*, vol. 2 (1980), p. 335.
25 Rainer Maria Rilke, letter to Clara Rilke of 25 February 1907, in *Letters of Rainer Maria Rilke, 1892–1910*, p. 264.
26 Rainer Maria Rilke, *The Notebooks of Malte Laurids Brigge*, trans. Michael Hulse (London: Penguin, 2016), p. 29 [translation slightly modified].
27 Ibid., p. 30.
28 Ibid., p. 60.
29 The fire is the one in *Ghosts*, the drowning is that of the child in *Little Eyolf*, the fall that of the architect in *The Master Builder*. As for the avalanche, it buries the characters of *When We Dead Awaken*.
30 Ibid., p. 61.
31 Ibid., p. 33.
32 Ibid., p. 575; cf. letter to Clara Rilke of 4 October 1907, in *Letters of Rainer Maria Rilke, 1892–1910*, p. 301.
33 See, 'The Last Supper', in *Rainer Maria Rilke: Selected Poems*, trans. Albert Ernest Flemming (Routledge: New York, 2011) p. 38.
34 Rilke, *The Notebooks of Malte Laurids Brigge*, p. 54.
35 Ibid., p. 57.
36 Ibid., p. 153.
37 Ibid., p. 28.
38 Letter to Lou Andreas Salomé, 18 July 1903, in *Letters of Rainer Maria Rilke, 1892–1910*, p. 110.
39 Rilke, *The Notebooks of Malte Laurids Brigge*, p. 28.
40 Ibid., p. 37.
41 Ibid., p. 37.

The Threshold of Science
1 Karl Marx, *Capital*, vol. 1, trans. Ben Fowkes (London: Penguin Books in association with New Left Review, 1976), p. 125.
2 Ibid., p. 131.
3 Ibid., p. 132.
4 Aristotle, *Poetics*, in *The Complete Works of Aristotle:*

The Revised Oxford Translation (Princeton, NJ: Princeton University Press, 1991), 1453a, 36–9.

5   Marx, *Capital*, vol. 1, p. 140.
6   Ibid., p. 200.
7   Ibid., pp. 279–80.
8   Ibid., pp. 811–12.
9   Ibid., pp. 364–5.
10 Ibid., p. 369.
11 Ibid., p. 371.
12 Ibid., p. 352.
13 Ibid., p. 875.
14 Ibid., p. 354.
15 Ibid., p. 359.
16 Ibid., pp. 842–3.
17 Ibid., p. 844.
18 'Letter from Marx to Engels, 10 February 1866', in Karl Marx and Friedrich Engels, *Letters on 'Capital'*, trans. Andrew Drummond (London: New Park Publications, 1983), p. 97.
19 Friedrich Engels, *The Condition of the Working Class in England*, ed. David McLellan (Oxford: Oxford University Press, 1999), pp. 312–25. [Translator's note: The passages to which Rancière is referring here are also to be found in Engels' preface to the English edition.]
20 Marx, *Capital*, vol. 1, p. 198.
21 Ibid., p. 786.
22 Ibid., p. 926.
23 Ibid., p. 928.
24 Ibid.
25 Ibid., p. 930.
26 Ibid., p. 929.
27 Edgar Allan Poe, 'The Murders in the Rue Morgue', in *Poetry and Tales* (New York: The Library of America, 1984), p. 401.
28 Honoré de Balzac, *Louis Lambert*, in *La Comédie humaine* (Paris: Gallimard 'Bibliothèque de la Pléiade'), vol. 11 (1980), p. 613.
29 Poe, 'The Murders in the Rue Morgue', pp. 403–4.

30 Régis Messac, *Le 'Detective Novel' et l'influence de la pensée scientifique* (Paris: Honoré Champion, 1929).

31 Edgar Allan Poe, 'The Philosophy of Composition', *Essays and Reviews* (New York: The Library of America, 1984), p. 13.

32 'As for Emma, she did not ask herself whether she loved him. Love, she thought, must come suddenly, with great outbursts and lightning, – a hurricane of the skies, which sweeps down on life, upsets everything, uproots the will like a leaf and carries away the heart as in an abyss. She did not know that on the terrace of houses rain makes lakes when the pipes are choked, and she would thus have remained safe in her ignorance when she suddenly discovered a rent in the wall.' Gustave Flaubert, *Madame Bovary*, trans. Eleanor Marx Aveling and Paul de Man (New York: W. W. Norton and Company, 2005), Part Two, chapter IV, p. 84.

33 Jorge Luis Borges, Prologue to Adolfo Bioy Casares, *The Invention of Morel*, trans. Ruth L. C. Simms (New York: New York Review Books, 2003), p. 40 (Spanish original, 1940).

34 Émile Gaboriau, *The Lerouge Case* (London: G. Heath Robinson & J. Birch, 1921), p. 24 [translation modified]. The scientist referred to here is, of course, Cuvier.

35 Conan Doyle, *A Study in Scarlet* (London: Macmillan Collector's Library, 2005), p. 29.

36 Ibid., p. 47.

37 Dashiell Hammett, *The Red Harvest* (New York & London: Knopf, 1929).

The Shores of the Real

1 Joseph Conrad, *Under Western Eyes* (Oxford: Oxford University Press, 2003), p. 3.

2 Borges, 'Prologue' to Casares, *The Invention of Morel*, p. 5.

3 Joseph Conrad, 'Guy de Maupassant', in *Notes on Life and Letters* (London: J. M. Dent and Sons, 1949), p. 31.

4 Joseph Conrad, *Lord Jim: A Tale* (Oxford: Oxford World's Classics, 2002), p. 306.

5 Letter to R. B. Cunninghame Graham, 31 October 1904, in *The Collected Letters of Joseph Conrad*, ed. L. Davies and J. H. Shape, Vol. 3 (Cambridge: Cambridge University Press, 2015), p. 175.

6 Joseph Conrad, *The Heart of Darkness and Other Tales* (Oxford: Oxford World's Classics, 2002), p. 161.

7 Ibid., p. 107.

8 Letter to R. B. Cunninghame Graham, 8 February 1899, in *The Collected Letters of Joseph Conrad*, Vol. 2, p. 160. [My translation – SC. The original is in French: 'hormis la fidelité à une cause absolument perdue, à une idée sans avenir'.]

9 Conrad, *Under Western Eyes*, p. 192.

10 Joseph Conrad, *The Secret Agent* (London: Oxford: Oxford World's Classics, 2012), p. 270.

11 Letter to F. Unwin, 22 July 1896, *The Collected Letters of Joseph Conrad*, Vol. 1, pp. 302–3.

12 W. G. Sebald, *The Rings of Saturn*, trans. Michael Hulse (New York: New Directions, 2016), p. 3.

13 Ibid., p. 9 [translation modified].

14 Ibid., p. 4.

15 Ibid., p. 3.

16 *The Emergence of Memory: Conversations with W. G. Sebald*, ed. Lynne Sharon Schwartz (New York: Seven Stories Press, 2007), p. 56.

17 W. G. Sebald, *On the Natural History of Destruction*, trans. Anthea Bell (New York: Random House, 2003), p. 91.

18 Ibid., p. 39.

19 Ibid., p. 40.

20 Sebald, *The Rings of Saturn*, p. 155.

21 Ibid., p. 237.

22 Ibid., p. 170.

23 Ibid., p. 151 [translation modified].

24 W. G. Sebald, *Vertigo*, trans. Michael Hulse (New York: New Directions, 2016), p. 73.

25 Sebald, *The Rings of Saturn*, p. 211.

26 Marx, *Capital*, vol. 1, p. 1044.

27 Sebald, *The Rings of Saturn*, p. 283 [translation modified].

28 W. G. Sebald, *A Place in the Country*, trans. Jo Caitling (London: Penguin, 2013), p. 17.

29 Sebald, *The Rings of Saturn*, pp. 45–6.

30 Sebald, *A Place in the Country*, pp. 17–19.

31 *The Emergence of Memory*, p. 106.

The Edge of the Nothing and the All

1 Georg Lukács, 'Narrate or Describe?', in *Writer and Critic and Other Essays*, ed. and trans. Arthur Kahn (London: Merlin Press, 1970), p. 144.

2 Auerbach, *Mimesis*, p. 552.

3 Ibid., p. 547.

4 Ibid., p. 548.

5 Aristotle, *Poetics*, 1453a, 10.

6 Auerbach, *Mimesis*, p. 554.

7 Flaubert, *Madame Bovary*, Part One, chapter IX, p. 56.

8 I've elaborated on this aspect of the novel in *The Lost Thread*.

9 William Faulkner, *The Sound and the Fury*, in *Faulkner: Novels 1926–1929* (New York: Library of America, 2006), p. 1098. See below, 'The Mute's Speech'.

10 William Faulkner, *Light in August*, in *Faulkner: Novels 1930–1935* (New York: The Library of America, 1985), p. 671.

11 Maurice Maeterlinck, 'Tragedy of Everyday Life', in *A Maeterlinck Reader*, ed. and trans. David Willinger and Daniel Gerould (New York: Peter Lang, 2011), p. 301 [translation modified].

12 Faulkner, *The Sound and the Fury*, p. 879.

13 Ibid., p. 1098.

14 Pierre-Simon Ballanche, *Première sécession de la plèbe* (Rennes: Pontcerq, 2017), p. 117.

15 João Guimarães Rosa, 'The Thin Edge of Happiness', in *The Third Bank of the River and Other Stories*, translated from the Portuguese and with an Introduction by Barbara Shelby (New York: Alfred A. Knopf, 1968).

16 'Treetops', ibid., p. 238 [translation modified].

17 Ibid., p. 236.

18 'In the sertão what can a person do with their free time

if not tell stories? The only difference is that, instead of recounting them, I write.' Conversation with Gunter Lorenz, in João Guimarães Rosa, *Ficção Completa*, vol. 1 (Rio de Janeiro: Nova Aguilar, 1994), p. 33.

19 Ibid., p. 35.

20 'Notorious', in *The Third Bank of the River and Other Stories*, p. 221.

21 'The Dagobé Brothers', ibid., p. 31.

22 'A young man, gleaming white', ibid., pp. 99–107.

23 'No Man, No Woman', ibid., p. 170.

24 Ibid., p. 171.

25 Ibid., p. 173.

26 'The Third Bank of the River', ibid., p. 190.

27 Ibid., p. 40.

28 Ibid., p. 41.

29 'Nothingness and the Human Condition', ibid., p. 123.

30 'Cause and Effect', ibid., p. 76.

31 Ibid., p. 180.

32 'Hocus Psychocus', ibid., p. 186.

33 'Soroco, His Mother, His Daughter', ibid., p. 217.

Index

Index

Index

Rousseau, Jean-Jacques 17
Reveries of a Solitary Walker
104

sado-masochism 35
São Paolo 117
Scheveningen 117
Schopenhauer, Arthur 39, 84,
93
scientific rationality 3, 6, 10,
52–3, 76–8
Sebald, W. G. 124
The Emigrants 107
A Place in the Country 122
The Rings of Saturn 103–11,
115–19, 120–2
Vertigo 118
sensible-suprasensible beings
56, 58
sensitive souls, communication
between 16–20, 28, 39
sertão 154, 157, 166
Shakespeare, William, *Macbeth*
145
signs 19, 35
inversion of meanings 83
science of 37, 82–4
silkworms 114, 120
social barriers 10, 13, 15–16
social relationships 6, 59
social science 3, 4–5, 7–8, 27
Somerleyton Hall 103,
112–13
Sophocles 36
Southwold 113, 116
space-time 134
speech, voiceless 145–51
Stendhal 7, 40
The Charterhouse of Parma
16–21, 39, 89
The Red and the Black 16,
132
supernatural 20
surface of things 36
surplus value 63–4, 120
suspense formula 155–6

suspension of disbelief 157
Swedenborg, Emanuel 76, 79
Swedenborgian spirituality 20,
76
Swinburne, Algernon 103
symbolist age 42
sympathy and antipathy 93–5,
101

telepathy 20–1
temporalities 130–4, 151–2
calendar time 121
cartography of time 121
of causality 6
chronicled time 6, 149
distinguishing of 3
dominant time 152
edge of time 136
empty time 132
fictional time 149
hierarchy of times 130–3
labour-time 54–5
outside-of-time 134, 156
of the realist novel 131
space-time 134
stolen time 54, 62–4
successive time 131
temporal disorder 145, 151
The Three Princes of Serendip
74
topography of fiction 14, 104,
111
tragedy 1, 5, 57, 83
Aristotelian 30, 83
bad tragedy 57
denouement 57, 78
equitable settlement 57
good tragedy 67
inversion of appearances 57,
83
'true life' 154, 158–61, 163–4
see also reality
'true' stories 156
see also realist fiction
truth 3, 37–40, 59, 82–3
see also verisimilitude